Soccer Drills

Complete Guide to Developing Your Soccer Moves

(Top Finishing Drills From the World's Best Soccer Clubs)

Lilian Goetz

Published By **Bella Frost**

Lilian Goetz

Soccer Drills: Complete Guide to Developing Your Soccer Moves (Top Finishing Drills From the World's Best Soccer Clubs)

ISBN   978-1-998769-56-8

No part of this guidebook shall be reproduced in any form without permission in writing from the publisher except in the case of brief quotations embodied in critical articles or reviews.

Legal & Disclaimer

from and against any damages, costs, and expenses, including any legal fees potentially resulting from the application of any of the information provided by this guide. This disclaimer applies to any damages or injury caused by the use and application, whether directly or indirectly, of any advice or information presented, whether for breach of contract, tort, negligence, personal injury, criminal intent, or under any other cause of action.

You agree to accept all risks of using the information presented inside this book. You need to consult a professional medical practitioner in order to ensure you are both able and healthy enough to participate in this program.

Table of contents

Chapter 1: Evolution of Football Strategy

American football has evolved into a complex game of strategy since the invention of the forward pass. Each year, coaches expand on the original principles in an attempt to find an advantage over their opponents. Football playbooks can be as thick as a dictionary on the college and professional levels. The innovations of offense and the defenses created to counteract each play can seem like quantum physics to someone new to the sport. Coaching strategies continue to evolve just as players continue to get bigger, stronger, and faster. Football is not just a game of strength, speed, and skill. It is also a chess match as coaches use combinations of formations and plays to help give their players the best chance to succeed.

There have been many coaches credited with changing the way the game is played through inventive schemes over the years. From three yards and a cloud of dust to today's pass happy spread offenses. Coaches have always looked for ways to get an edge on opposing defenses. Innovations like the T-Formation, the single wing, "Air Coryell", all changed the game at one time. Throwbacks like the wildcat offense put a twist on older principles. All of these offensive philosophies were innovative at one time or another. Offenses are constantly changing causing defenses to figure out new ways to defend them.

The defensive side of the football has seen just as many changes. Defenses like the forty-six defense, "Tampa Two", and sophisticated zone blitz schemes are some of the many principles designed to make life difficult for opposing offenses. Defensive coordinators work just as hard as their offensive counterparts to dictate the pace of the game. Modern day defenses don't only strive to stop their opponents from scoring, they actually want to score points themselves. The strategic aspect of football is becoming just as important as the physical part of the game.

What are the formations offenses use and why? What do defenses do to combat these ideas? What is effective in the game of football and what can teams do to stop it? These are some of the questions that will be answered later on in this book. This guide will help you understand how an "X" and an "O" on a chalkboard can translate into elaborate schemes.

Chapter 2: Creating a Scheme

There are hundreds of combinations of offensive and defensive plays that can be run from many different formations in the game of football. In order to have an effective strategy, a team needs to develop a scheme. A scheme is the basic principles in which an offense or defense will use to be successful. Play calling is not a random thing. Each play is intended to build off other plays in order to make the next play more effective. Explosive plays are the reason people enjoy the game of football, and they cannot be executed if a proper scheme is not created. Each play ran during the course of the game should have a purpose in the overall scheme.

There are two basic types of plays an offense can run. A rushing play and a passing play. There are hundreds of variations to each type of play, but each play falls into one of the two categories. Either the play is designed to be a passing play or a running play. Mixing these two types of plays effectively is one of the keys to a good offense. The goal is to confuse the defense to make it harder for them to stop you. The odds of being successful are elevated when the defense has no idea what the offense is attempting to do.

Rushing plays are usually low risk low reward plays. The goal of rushing plays is to consistently move the ball forward with smaller risks of negative plays or turnovers. Rushing plays require blocking schemes to be nearly perfect in order to gain large amounts of yards on one play. On the flip side, the risk of things going wrong on these plays are less. Rushing plays are also more effective at picking up short yards. It is easier to find players who can be effective runners than it is to find players who can be effective as passers.

Passing plays are higher risk, but have higher chances at gaining large amounts of yardage at one time. The ball travels in the air on these plays so there is a better chance to get the ball into the hands of a player in open space. Having the ball in open spaces increases the chance that player can get a lot of yards at once and possible score a touchdown. With this increase in efficiency also comes an increase of risk. Defensive players have an opportunity to catch the ball just like the offensive player does which increases the risk of turnovers. There is also the chance that no one will catch the ball and no yards will be gained on the play.

There are three basic types of plays on defense. The first is man to man defense. Just like the name implies, this type of coverage is when a player is responsible for defending another player. This is an aggressive brand of coverage that gives the defense a chance of making big plays. Having defenders who can match up man to man also allows a coach to be more aggressive with blitzing. However, man to man defense involves risk. If the defender is beat on a play, there may not be anyone else in the area close enough to help. This type of play requires talented defenders who can win individual plays against their offensive counterparts.

The second type of defensive play is zone coverage. The basic principle of zone coverage is that defensive players defend an area of the field rather than a person. This player stays in their zone even if the closes offensive player leaves the zone. It requires the trust in your teammates to know they are going to have the next area covered. This type of defense works well when you don't have the most athletic players who may not be able to compete individually against quicker offensive players. Zone defense allows other defenders to fill into an area to make tackles once the ball crosses the line of scrimmage because all the defenders in the zone are typically facing the offense and can see everything in front of them.

The third type of defensive play is the blitz. This form of defense is most effective at stopping rushing plays, but can also be used to aggressively pressure passing plays. The point of the blitz is to send players toward the line of scrimmage at the snap of the ball. This form of defense forces the offense to react rather than dictate the flow of the game. Being this aggressive on defense can have high rewards, but also carries large risks. Blitzing plays can cause the offense to make mistakes, but it increases the risk of big plays for the offense as failed blitzes can put defensive players in bad situations if the offense is ready for it.

Chapter 3: Offensive Formations

Offenses can use many formations during the course of a game. The basic requirement of an offensive formation is that seven players must line up on the line of scrimmage and someone must be behind the center to receive the snap. Outside of that, players can be in many different areas on the field. Some of the most used offensive formations are the I-Formation, the split back or pro-set, single back formation, the spread formation, and the shotgun formation. There are many variations to each of these formation depending on personnel on the field, but these are the basics used mostly today.

The I-Formation is one of the basic formations used in football. This formation is created when the quarterback lines up under center with both a fullback and a tailback behind him. The tailback is normally behind the fullback. It is common to run out of this formation with the fullback leading the tailback into the hole created by the offensive line. With normal personnel, there are two wide receivers, a tight end, and five offensive linemen in front of the backs. However, the number of receivers and tight ends can be changed in this formation.

The pro-set formation is a variation of the I-Formation where the two backs are split on either side behind the quarterback. This formation is similar to the I-Formation in terms of personnel and the types of plays that can be run out of it. Both passing and rushing options exist in this formation. However, this formation has some tradeoffs compared to the I-Formation. The fullback is less of a threat to block in this formation since he is lined up on one side of the formation. However, the pro-set formation creates more uncertainty for the defense in terms of reading the direction the ball is going.

The single back formation removes the fullback and substitutes an extra receiver or tight end. This type of formation allows both passing and rushing plays. The removal of the fullback takes away a blocker, but allows more speed or skilled players on the field. The single back formation adds more options to the passing game by adding another skilled route runner. This formation and personnel will normally cause the defense to adjust their personnel to react to the offensive play call.

The spread formation has become a staple in college offenses as well as some professional teams. The spread formation is an aggressive form of offense where the receivers are spread out wide along the line of scrimmage. An offense can use as many as five wide receivers in this offense and it is predominantly used for passing. However, rushing plays are possible. The fact the defense has to spread out to cover all the receivers can sometimes leave holes for a running back, or sometimes an athletic, quarterback to gain large chunks of yardage.

The shotgun formation is formed when the quarterback stands about five yards behind the center and receives the snap through the air rather than having the ball handed to him by the center. This formation usually has one running back, but can have other variations such as the quarterback lining up in the backfield alone. In the traditional shotgun formation, the running back normally lines up next to the quarterback. The shotgun formation is mostly used for passing, but rushing plays are also possible. The advantage of this form of offense is the quarterback is further away from the defense when the play starts. This gives the quarterback extra time to read the defense and get rid of the ball before the pass rush can get to him.

These are some of the most commonly used offensive formations deployed in football. The list of formations and plays continue to grow as coaches continue to look for creative ways to be successful. The more creativity that exists on the offensive side of the ball, the more sophisticated defenses have to be to combat these plays. Defenses have their own defensive formations used to stop the offensive playbook.

Chapter 4: Base Defenses

Much like offensive play calls, the defensive coaches have their own formations used during the course of the game. A defense normally has a base defense, then substitution packages based on what personnel the offense has on the field. The base defenses used the most in today's game are the three-four defense and the four-three defense. The difference between two defensive formations is the players on the field. The three-four alignment has three defensive linemen and four linebackers. The four-three defensive formation has four defensive linemen and three linebackers. Another alternative is a hybrid base defense that uses both three-four and four-three sets in order to create uncertainty for the offense.

The three-four defensive alignment has three down linemen, four linebackers, and four defensive backs. This alignment normally consists of two defensive ends with a defensive tackle lined up at the line of scrimmage. The defensive tackle in a three-four defense is often called a nose tackle or nose guard because they normally line up on the nose of the offensive center. There are two outside linebackers and two inside linebackers behind the defensive line along with four defensive backs. The key to this defensive formation is to create confusion in the offense. Having four athletic linebackers on the field gives the coach many options in play calling.

The four-three defense has four down linemen, three linebackers, and four defensive backs. This alignment normally has two defensive ends and two defensive tackles on the line of scrimmage. A four-three defensive has three linebackers often referred to as the strong side linebacker, middle linebacker, and weak side linebacker. The strong side linebacker is lined up on the strong side of the offense. This means the strong side linebacker will line up on the side of the field where the offense has the most personnel. The middle linebacker aligns in the middle of the field and the weak side linebacker lines up on the side of the field with the least number of offensive players.

There are many reasons coaches decide between these two base defenses. A lot of it depends on the defensive personnel. A three-four require bigger and stronger personnel while a four-three usually needs smaller faster players. In a three-four, three defensive linemen line up against five offensive linemen.

The nose guard is constantly required to take on two blockers. All defensive linemen and linebackers in a three-four need to be stronger than there four-three counterparts because they are expected to shed blockers.

A four-three defense requires more athletic defensive linemen. Three-four defensive lineman primarily work to engage blockers with strength in order to free up linebackers to make a play. Four-three defensive linemen are expected to beat blockers and get up feel to stop rushing plays and pressure the quarterback on passing plays. Both formations will use similar plays, it's mostly a matter of personnel and responsibilities which makes the difference between the two alignments.

Defenses will also use substitution packages in passing situations. These packages include the nickel and dime defenses. The nickel is created when a linebacker is removed from a formation and replaced by a defensive back. The fifth defensive back creates a nickel formation. Substituting a sixth defensive back creates a dime formation. These packages help defend multiple wide receiver formations an offense may run.

Chapter 5: Offensive Philosophy Verses

Defensive Philosophy

Coaches must choose if their offense will be run based, pass based, or a balance between the two. Different variations of formations can be used depending on what the offense is trying to accomplish. If the team will be run based, they will normally use fullbacks and multiple tight end sets because these players are often better blockers. Offenses that prefer to pass more often will use formations with multiple wide receiver because they are quicker and have better catching abilities. Teams with a balance attack will use multiple formations and personnel to try and create matchups.

Run based offenses will use a lot of I-Formation or single back formations. A lot of modern offenses substitute a fullback for an H-Back or tight end. Often times the H-Back or a tight end will be more athletic than a traditional fullback. Run based offenses can use variations of the I formation by using multiple tight ends and moving them around the formation. The I-Formation is considered a power formation where the offense tries to physically control the line of scrimmage to create running lanes. This is one of the most commonly used formations in football.

Offenses that are heavily based on rushing plays try to use size as strength to impose their will on the defense. Normally, these teams require strong offensive linemen, tight ends, and fullbacks in addition to a talented running back. It is important for teams to have strong run blockers to create space for the running back to operate. It is also important for the running back to have the vision to find open space and the ability to make defenders miss in one on one situations. On most plays, there are only nine available blockers as quarterbacks are not often called upon to block. So that leaves two free defenders who may possibly be in position to make a tackle. It is sometimes up to the running back to make these players miss to pick up more yardage.

Defenses will attempt to defend most I-Formation plays in their base defense. Both a three-four and a four-three defense can match up against the base personnel for the offense. There are two different ways a defense can decide to attack the I-Formation. A defense can be a one gap or a two gap defense. Either of these philosophies work, it is just a matter of how a coach chooses to defend the run.

A one gap defense is executed just as it sounds. Each player is responsible for one gap on the field. For example, a defense end in a four-three defense may be responsible for the gap between the offensive left tackle and left guard. This means the defensive end in this situation must win this spot on the field and tackle the ball carrier if the play is coming in this gap. If the ball carrier goes into a different gap, the defensive end will keep containment in his gap. However, he is no longer responsible for the ball carrier. The defensive end in this example should not vacate his fit in the defense and will rely on the teammate who is covering the next gap. This philosophy allows defenders to be very aggressive coming off the ball to get into their gaps.

Chapter 6: Specialty Defensive Package

There are situations when a base three-four or four-three will not work. Both of these defensive formations have four defensive backs behind the front seven. This formation will have difficulty defending multiple wide receiver sets since most linebackers are not fast enough to defend wide receivers. Defenses must substitute extra defensive backs to cover the extra speed introduced by the wide receivers. These sub packages exist in both three-four bases as well as four-three bases.

A nickel defense is a sub package where a fifth defensive back is substituted for a linebacker or defensive lineman. This fifth defensive back will usually be on the field when the offense has three or more wide receivers. The formation strengthens the pass coverage of a defense by adding a quicker more athletic defender to defend in passing situations. The disadvantage of this package is that the defensive back is normally smaller than and not as strong as the linebacker he replaces. Therefore, the defense is not as strong against the run in a nickel formation as opposed to the based defense.

A dime defense is a sub package where a sixth defensive back is substituted for another linebacker or defensive lineman. This extra defensive back is used in four and five receiver sets. The dime package of defense is very quick, but does not have the tackling ability of the base defense. A dime defense gives a defense the best opportunity to defend a pass, but is the least effective against running plays.

The nickel and dime formations are used to defend multiple receiver sets. Without these formations, offenses would be able to pass the ball against base defenses without much trouble. Most linebackers just don't have the ability to defend wide receivers. Being able to substitute extra defensive backs gives defenses a way to combat offensive substitutions.

Chapter 7: Other Offensive Strategies

Offenses use ways other than formations to confuse defenses. There are other strategies deployed to try and take advantages of defensive strategy. The offense controls the ball and can use different ideas and principles to gain an advantage by manipulating the defense. These devices are often used during the course of a football game to figure out the best way to attack a defense and score as many points as possible.

Offenses will use shifts to gain an advantage against a defense. A shift is when players move to a different position and reset before the quarterback receives a snap from the center. For example, a team may line up in a single back set with two wide receivers and two tight ends. One of the tight ends may shift into the backfield and create an I-Formation. This shift can cause a matchup issue for the defense. The defense has to try to diagnose if what looked like a passing formation may have just adjusted into a running formation. Perhaps it is still a passing formation. The defense must react to this play based on what happened after they have already made their defensive play call.

Motion is another tool offenses use to gain an advantage against the defense. The difference between a shift and motion is the players moving and the timing. In most rulebooks, only one player is allowed to go in motion at one time while many players can shift at one. Shifts occur before the snap of the ball while motion can continue as the ball is snapped. Shifting players must come to a complete stop and reset at a new position before the ball can be snapped while a player in motion does not have to reset. However, the player in motion cannot be moving toward the line of scrimmage at the snap of the ball.

Shifts and motion both serve another purpose for the offense. It allows offensive players to read what the defense wants to do before the snap of the ball. A defense has to react to a player moving before the snap of the ball. How the defense reacts to these situations can tell the offense a lot about what kind of play the defense is in.

An offense may start out in a single back formation then motions the back out of the backfield into a flanker position. The reaction of the defense tells the offense what kind of defense their opponent is playing. If a linebacker moves with the running back, the defense is probably in man to man coverage. If the defense does not react to the running back, they are probably in zone defense so they don't have to worry about matching up with the player. The defense is defending areas of the field so having that player into a new zone doesn't affect what the defense is trying to do.

Another way an offense attempts to affect the defense is with hurry up or no huddle offense. This form of offense occurs when a team goes back to the line of scrimmage immediately at the conclusion of the previous play. The quarterback calls the plays at the line of scrimmage based on the way the defense is aligned. This form of offense does not allow defenses a chance to make substitutions in between plays.

Chapter 8: Other Defensive Strategies

Defensive coaches also use strategies to confuse the offensive players. One of the ways defenses attack an offense is through blitzing. A blitz is when a defense aggressively send players toward the offense in hopes of disrupting an offensive play. The goal of a blitz is to send more players in one area than an offense can block. The confusion is in the disguise. The key is to find ways to hide what players are blitzing to decrease the chances the offense will be able to get that player or players blocked.

Blitzing the pass is a way of disrupting the timing of an offensive play. The goal is to pressure the quarterback to either sack or cause the quarterback to make a mistake. Blitzing is a high risk high reward play. There is a good chance to disrupt the offense on a blitz, but if it is not affective, the defense will be exposed to possible big plays against them.

One of the ways coaches disguise blitzes is to utilize zone blitzes. This is when a player who would normally attack the line of scrimmage actually falls back into coverage and is replaced by a player who would not normally blitz. An example of a zone blitz would be in a three-four formation. On a typical passing play in a three-four defense, all three defensive linemen would rush the passer along with one of the four linebackers. The other seven defenders would drop into coverage. During a zone blitz, one of the defensive ends would drop back into zone coverage while the outside and inside linebackers on his side would rush the quarterback. This design is created to confuse the quarterback into thinking all three players are rushing the quarterback. In this example, the quarterback may attempt to throw the ball quickly into the area where the blitzing linebackers are vacating. However, the defensive end may be in position to intercept the ball if he is able to drop back into the area where the quarterback is throwing the ball.

Sometimes coaches will fake blitzes in order to confuse the pass protection. An example in a four-three defense would be if the middle linebacker and the strong side linebacker both walked up to the line of scrimmage. Each players would stand at the line of scrimmage in one of the gaps between the center and a guard. This pre-play formation would lead the offence to believe the players will be blitzing. The offensive line now has to account for these players and try to block them. When the quarterback snaps the ball, both linebackers fall back into coverage rather than blitzing. The confusion at the line can open holes for the defensive linemen to rush the quarterback. A properly executed fake can lead to quarterback sacks as well as turnovers if a quarterback rushes the pass.

These are some of the ways defenses try to confuse offensive players. A lot of the strategies deployed during the course of the game go on after the original play call is created. Teams can use different strategies to try and gain an advantage over their opponents. These are the games within the game that happen during the course of four quarters.

Chapter 9: Offensive and Defensive

Adjustments

The basic rule of offensive football is to gain ten yards in three plays in order to get a first down. As mentioned earlier, running the football is a good way to consistently pick up short amounts of yards. An offence can be very successful if they can run the ball for four or five yards on each attempt. This would lead to first downs and eventually touchdowns. It is very difficult for a defense to be successful if it cannot stop an offense's rushing attack.

In base offense versus base defense, the offense uses five offensive lineman, a tight end, and a fullback to block the front seven in either a four-three or a three-four. This is an important aspect of rushing plays in football. If the offense finds success running in these situations, the defense is forced to react. If a defense can stop the offence in this situation, the offense becomes one dimensional and has to pass more often than they would like to. This battle is one of the most simplistic, but important aspects of a football game.

When the defense struggles at stopping the offense in seven on seven, they have to commit other resources to stop the run. The defense may then be forced to add an eighth man to the run stopping scheme. This is referred to as an eight man box. The eighth man is normally unaccounted which means they are not usually blocked. This formation is typically created when the defense uses a defensive back, usually a strong safety, to stop the run. The strong safety lines up closer to the line of scrimmage and serves almost as a fourth linebacker in a typical four-three or a fifth linebacker in a three-four. Having a strong safety closer to the line of scrimmage makes it harder for offenses to effectively block running plays because they simply do not have the number of blockers needed.

To counter act the eighth man, the offense can utilize play action passes. These plays are disguised as running plays, but are actually passing plays. The offense runs a play that originally looks like a rushing play and the quarterback pretends to hand the ball to the running back. The quarterback keeps the ball and then passes it to a receiver, tight end, or to a running back. The purpose of the play action pass is to get the defense to guess the offense is using a running play and have the defense move toward the line of scrimmage to stop it. The quarterback throws the ball behind them for a big play. A defense that cannot stop the run effectively without using an eight man box is susceptible to the play action pass.

TECHNICAL SEQUENCES

Exercise age difficulty
1U9+

   Theme : TECHNICAL EXERCISE

Players duration equipment
8
10 Balls, discs.

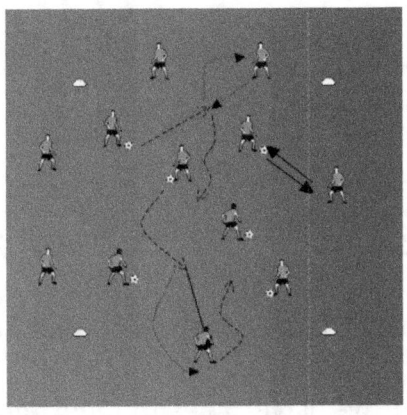

Explanations

Surface area of 20x20m. Place one or two play - ers on each side of the field (outside). The other players are inside the field and each have a ball.

27

The players dribble the ball and perform a technical sequence requested by the coach. If the action so requires, the player takes the place of the outside player and vice versa.

VARIATIONS

• Pass then the outside player dribbles past the passer
  • Red passes to a blue who passes to another blue who gives the ball back to Red
  • Red supports and passes to Blue then Red lets the ball pass between his legs and turns around to continue

Objectives

•	Varied technical	work
•		Dribbling
•		Pass
•	First	touch
•	One touch	play

INSTRUCTIONS
  • Pass
• Support and pass, then leave the ball to the outside player
• Screen: the player goes to meet the ball carrier
  • 1-2

information gathering

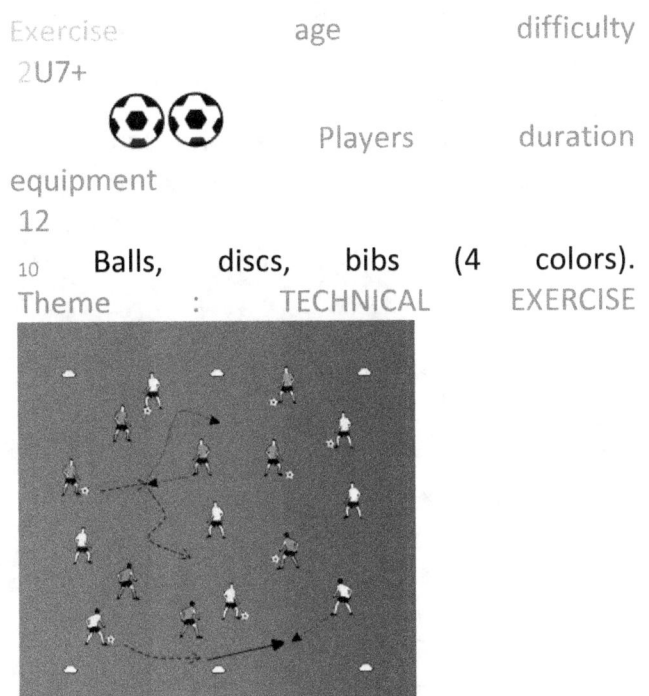

Explanations

Surface area of 25x25m. Make 4 teams. One ball for 2 players per team.
The players dribble the ball and try to pass it in good conditions to a moving partner. It can be a pass or a screen made with a partner who came to meet him.

Objectives

• Dribbling

29

- Pass
- Information gathering
- First touch

INSTRUCTIONS

- Only pass to players on your team
- Non-ball carriers move around to offer passing solutions
- Use both feet

VARIATIONS

• Pass only to a player positioned at least 5m away from you

• Find a solution with 4 ball touches maximum

• Do not give to a player on your team

BALL MOVEMENT

Exercise	age	difficulty
3 U9+		

Theme : TECHNICAL

EXERCISE

Players	duration	equipment
8		

Balls, discs, bibs (2 colors).

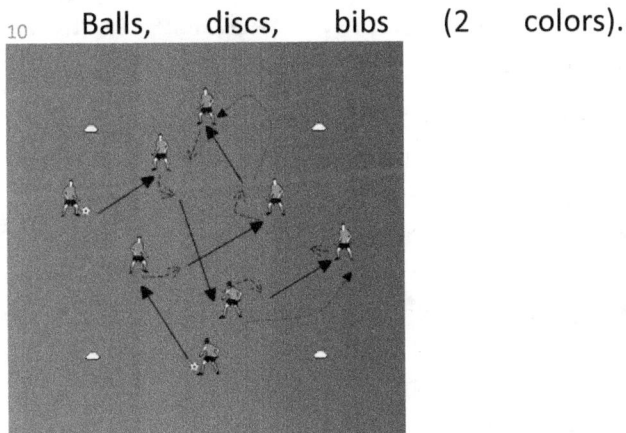

Explanations

Surface area of 20x20m. Two teams of 4 play
- ers each with a ball.
 Two players from each team stand on
opposite sides of the field (outside). Each
team passes the ball from one outside player
to the other via the middle players.

Objectives

- First   touch
- Pass
- Information   gathering

INSTRUCTIONS
- 2 ball touches: oriented control + pass
- The player who passes to the outside partner
replaces   him
- Pay attention to the opposing team's ball

31

- Fast and accurate technical sequences
VARIATIONS

- The outside players stays put and plays in support of the player who passes the ball to them
- Play with a single touch of the ball: offer passing solutions by moving to open spaces
- Add a third team: hexagon-shaped field

Tennis-ball

Exercise	age	difficulty
4	U13+	

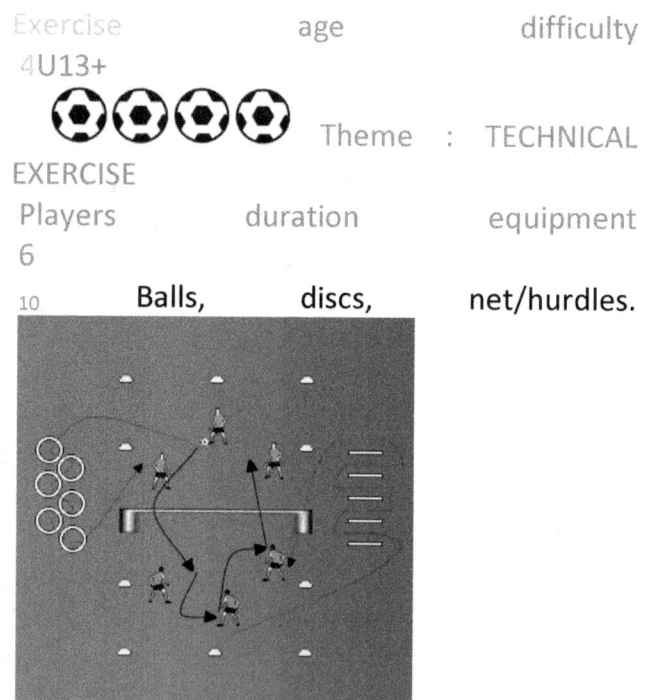

Theme : TECHNICAL EXERCISE

Players	duration	equipment
6	10	Balls, discs, net/hurdles.

Explanations

Surface area of 12x6m divided in two by a net. Two coordination stations on both sides of the field.

3 vs 3. After a sequence, the player will do one of the 2 coordination stations and then come back into play.

Objectives

- Finesse ball touch
- Control of a lifted pass
- Coordination
- Foot work

INSTRUCTIONS

- 1 rebound is allowed
- Play as in volleyball: a maximum of 2 passes before sending the ball back
- Play with a single touch of the ball
- Stations: 1 step in the hoops; side stepping between the bars

VARIATIONS

- Change the stations: 2 steps per hoop; 2 steps between the bars; etc.
- Play with 2 ball touches

Give and go with coordination (1)

Exercise	age	difficulty
5	U11+	

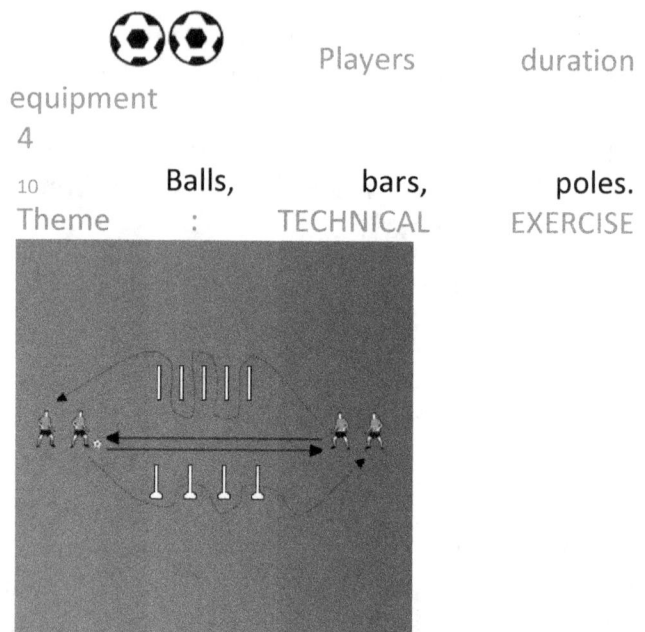

Explanations

In groups of 4 players with 1 ball for 4.
Pass and cut. The player passes the ball and goes to the coordination station before going behind the last player on the other side.
The player who receives the ball controls it then passes to the opposite side before doing the coordination station.

VARIATIONS

• 2 ball touches: firs touch + pass
• Play with a single touch of the ball
• Vary the coordination stations: 2 steps between the bars, backward side stepping,

one step in each hoop, touch the top of the cones, etc.

Objectives

- Quick control + pass sequence
- Foot work
- Coordination

INSTRUCTIONS
- Dribble between the poles
- Shuffle between the bars

1-touch give and go

Exercise	age	difficulty
6U11+		

	Theme	:	TECHNICAL
EXERCISE			

Players	duration	equipment
6		
10	Balls,	échelles.

Explanations

In groups of 6 players with 1 ball for 6. Pass and cut. The player passes the ball and does the footwork requested by the coach on the ladder before going behind the last player on the opposite side.

The player who receives the ball, passes

with- out controlling to the next player and then goes through the coordination ladder.

Objectives

- 1-touch pass
- Foot work
- Coordination

INSTRUCTIONS
- Play with a single touch of the ball
- Be ready to attack the ball
- Make 2 quick steps in each space of the ladder

VARIATIONS

- 1 step in each space
- 2 lateral steps in each space
- 2 ball touches: control + pass

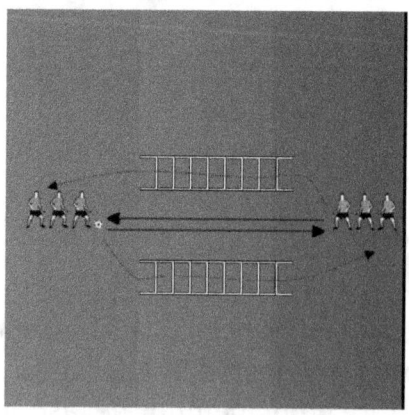

give and go with coordination (2)

⚽⚽⚽⚽ 8 Theme : TECHNICAL EXERCISE

duration   equipment

10 **Balls, poles, bars, cones, hoops.**

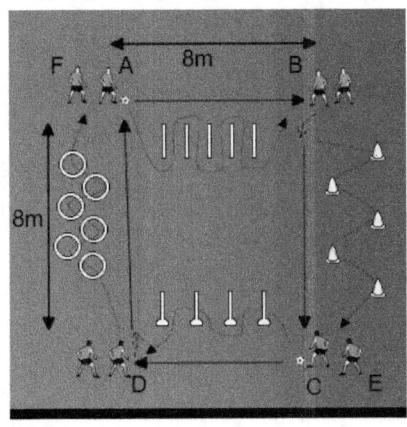

Explanations

Groups of at least 8 players.

Set up the stations as shown in the picture. A passes to B who controls and passes to E. At the same time, C passes to D who controls and passes to F.

After passing, the players go to the coordination station before moving on to the next station.

Objectives

37

- Quick control + pass sequence
- Foot work
- Coordination

INSTRUCTIONS

- 1 step in each hoop
- Shuffle between the bars
- Touch the top of each cone
- Dribble around the poles

VARIATIONS

• Give and go the other way: A passes to B and goes toward the station near D
• Change the drills to do at the stations: backward side stepping, slalom between the cones, 2 steps between the bars, etc.
• Change the stations

DRIBBLING AND PASSING SEQUENCE

Exercise age difficulty
8U9+

Players duration
equipment
6
10 Balls, discs.

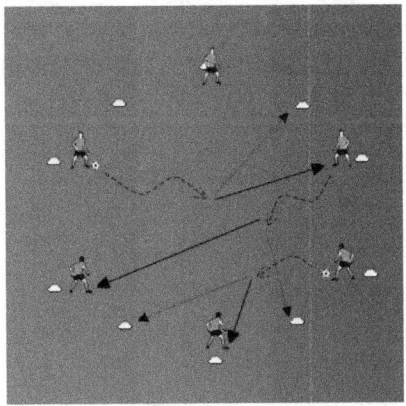

Explanations

In groups of 6 players with 2 balls. Place the discs as shown in the image. The players form a 12m diameter circle.
A player with a ball dribbles and passes to a player without a ball and stands in front of a free disc.

Objectives

- Dribbling   +   Pass
- Coordination
- Fakes

INSTRUCTIONS
• Start the game with 1 ball and then play with 2 and then 3 balls

• After passing, the gets back into his initial po - sition by shuffle, knees up, heels to buttocks, defensive steps, cross steps, etc.

VARIATIONS

• Perform a fake before the pass
• 2 ball touches: control + pass
• A player without a ball asks for the ball when he enters the circle

First touch and Pass

Exercise age difficulty Players
9 U11+

 8 Theme : TECHNICAL
EXERCISE
duration equipment
10 Balls, discs.

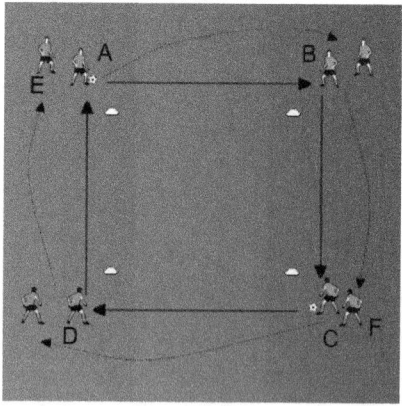

Explanations

15x15m square. The players are 2m away from the disc outside the square.

A passes to B who passes to C with a touch of the ball. At the same time, C passes to D who gives to E.

After their pass, the players move to the next disc.

Objectives

- Pass
- One touch play
- Quick control + pass sequence

INSTRUCTIONS
- Receive the ball outside the square
- Play with a single touch of the ball if possible
- Focus on pass quality

VARIATIONS
- Pass in one direction and run in the opposite direction
- 2 quick ball touches: first touch + pass

Dribbling, Passing and coordination

Exercise age difficulty

10 U9+

Players duration equipment

41

10 **Balls, discs, cones, bars, hoops.**

Theme : TECHNICAL EXERCISE

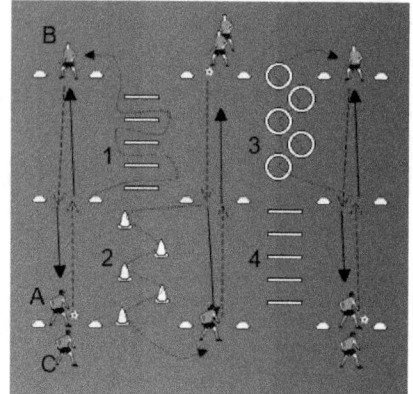

Explanations

In groups of 3 players with one ball for 3.
Set up coordination stations between each groups, as shown in the picture.
A dribbles the ball, passes to B and then goes through the station before going to B.
B dribbles and passes to C before going through the coordination station and going to C.

Objectives

- Dribbling
- Pass
- Foot work
- Coordination

INSTRUCTIONS

- 1 : shuffle
- 2 : touch the top of the cones
- 3 : 1 step per hoop
- 4 : 2 quick steps between each bar

VARIATIONS

- Change the coordination stations
- Add a fake before the pass

TEAM JUGGLING

Exercise age difficulty

11 U13+

Theme : TECHNICAL EXERCISE

Players duration equipment

6

10 Balls, discs, poles.

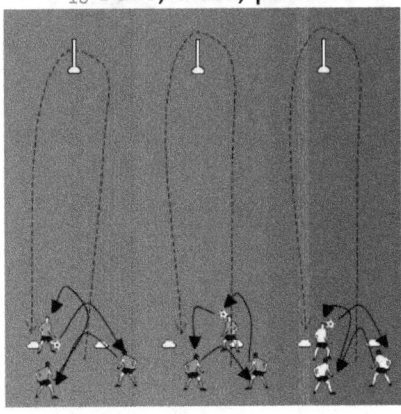

Explanations

43

Teams of 3 players with 1 ball per team.
The teams stand behind the starting line.
Place one pole per team 20m away from the starting line.
Teams must keep the ball in the air, walk around their pole and return to the starting line without dropping the ball.

Objectives

- Finesse ball touch
- Teamwork

INSTRUCTIONS
- Maximum 3 ball touches per player
- If the ball falls, return to the starting line and start again

VARIATIONS

- 1 ball touch
- Use specific body parts (right foot, left foot, head)
- Same drill but with 2, 4 or 5 players

Ball control (1)

12 U7+

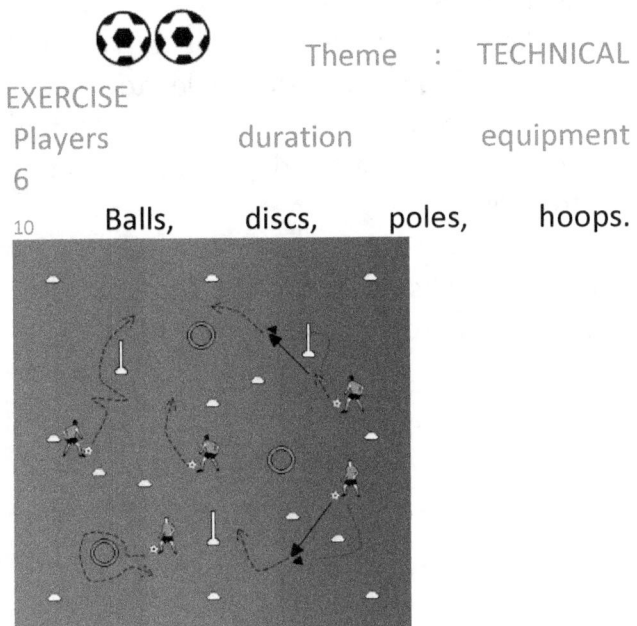

Theme : TECHNICAL EXERCISE

Players   duration   equipment

6

10   Balls,   discs,   poles,   hoops.

Explanations

20x20m surface area with some poles, hoops and 2m doors.
Each player dribbles a ball.
Players score a point each time they correctly perform a technical dribble in front of an ob- stacle.

Objectives

- Dribbling
- Ball control
- Pass
- 1 vs 1 moves

INSTRUCTIONS
- Make a move to beat a pole
- Kick the ball past the pole to beat it
- Nutmeg the doors
- Dribble around the hoops

VARIATIONS
- Use right and left foot
- Add other obstacles: avoid a forest of discs, pass under a hurdle and jump over it, etc.

ball Transmission

Exercise age difficulty

13 U9+

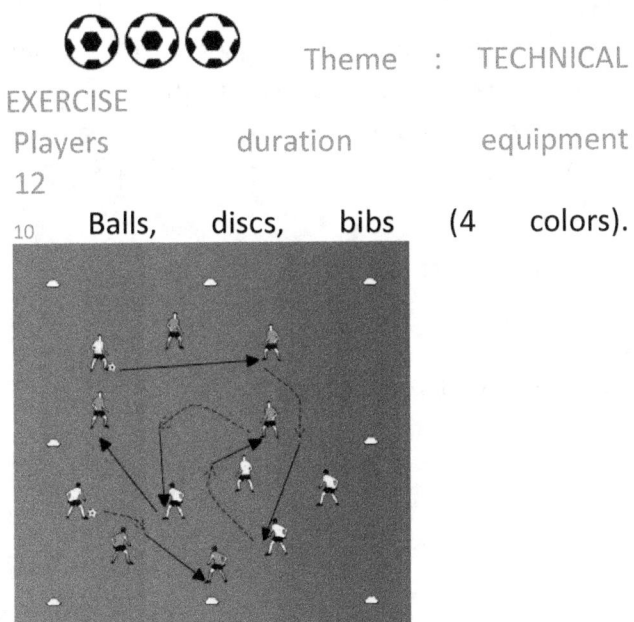

Theme : TECHNICAL EXERCISE

Players   duration   equipment

12

10   Balls,   discs,   bibs   (4   colors).

Explanations

Surface area of 25x25m. Four groups of play -
ers of different colors (4 colors).
Put 1 then 2 and finally 3 balls in play.
The players pass the balls in a specific order.

Objectives

-                                   Dribbling
-                                      Pass
-         Information   gathering
-     Make   yourself   available

INSTRUCTIONS

- A yellow always passes to a blue
- A blue always passes to a white
- A white always passes to a red
- A red always passes to a yellow

VARIATIONS

• Dribble the ball right up to the player's feet
• Pass the ball at least 5 meters away from the player
• Vary the passing order

Dribbling and Pass (1)

Exercise age difficulty

14 U9+

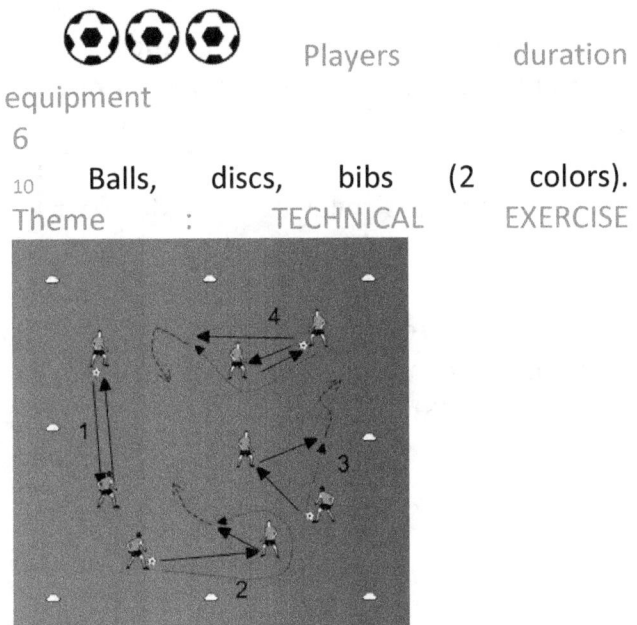

Players   duration

equipment

6

10   Balls,   discs,   bibs   (2   colors).
Theme   :   TECHNICAL   EXERCISE

Explanations

Surface area of 20x20m. Form 2 teams.
 The blues each have a ball and the reds don't
have a ball.
 Blue and red move around the field and
follow the orders of the coach. Switch roles
every 3 minutes.

Objectives

- Dribbling
- Pass
- One-two
- Support and pass

INSTRUCTIONS

- 1 : support and pass
- 2 : Blue passes to Red, runs behind him and Red makes a lead pass to Blue
- 3 : one-two
- 4 : support pass followed by a kick past Red to beat him

VARIATIONS

- Add other sequence: Blue nutmegs Red, screen between the 2 players, Blue beats Red with a dribble (Red is passive)

3-MAN play

Exercise age difficulty

15 U13+

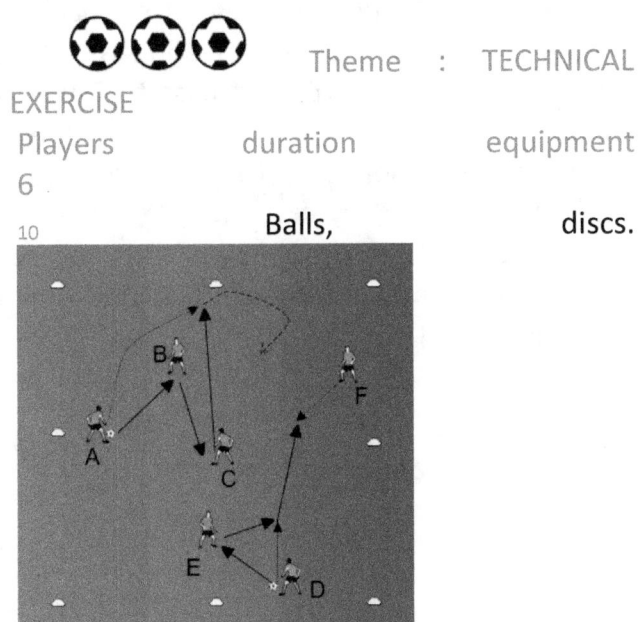

Theme : TECHNICAL EXERCISE

Players	duration	equipment
6	10	Balls, discs.

Explanations

Form groups of 3 players with a ball for 3.
The players play on the field while maintaining control of the ball.
They do the combination of passes ordered by the coach.

Objectives

- 3-man play
- Pass combination
- Off ball movement to offer solutions

INSTRUCTIONS

- A passes to B and runs behind his back. B passes to C who makes a lead pass to A
- 1-2 between D and E then pass to F who's running deep
- Support and then pass to the third player

VARIATIONS

- Other combinations of passes
- Put 3 mini-goals on the field: end the 3-man game with a goal

TECHNICAL DRILLS

Exercise age difficulty

16 U7+

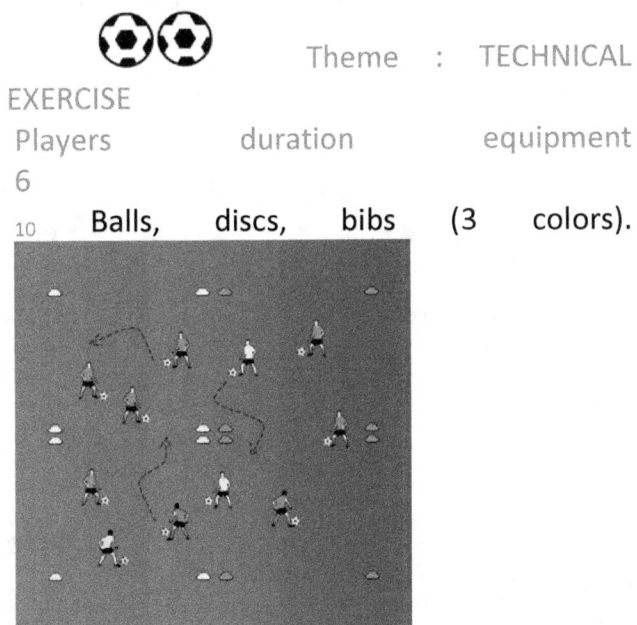

Theme : TECHNICAL EXERCISE

Players   duration   equipment

6

10   **Balls,   discs,   bibs**   (3   colors).

Explanations

Surface area of 20x20m divided into 4 areas. Every player has a ball. Divide players into 3 colors.
 The players move around the field and follow the instructions given by the coach.

VARIATIONS

• Dribble only in the white area (same as other colors)

• Players of the same color must dribble their ball behind each other and move from one area to the other

• Quick dribbling to avoid other players; etc.

Objectives

•			Dribbling
•	1	vs 1	moves
•	Change	of	pace

INSTRUCTIONS

• Dribble with the right foot, then the left, then the sole, etc.

• At the whistle, exchange the ball with anoth - er player (then only with a player of the same color)

• Kick the ball past another player to beat him

• Stop the ball in one area and recover a ball in another (if possible)

1 vs 1 moves and Pass

17 U9+

⚽⚽ 6 Theme : TECHNICAL

EXERCISE

duration   equipment

10 Balls, discs, 1 pole, 2 mini-goals.

Explanations

Groups of 6 players with 2 mini-goals.
Dribble the ball, beat the pole with a dribble and then shoot on goal. B does the same on the other side. C and D collect the balls from the goals and do the same.
A and B go back behind the opposite line.

Objectives

55

- Dribbling
- 1 vs 1 moves
- Passing/Shooting

INSTRUCTIONS

- Work on the different dribbling techniques (Faking, hooks, rakes)
- Fast 1 vs 1 moves + pass sequence
- Gradually passing the ball with more power
- 1 point per goal scored

VARIATIONS

- After dribbling in front of pole, A passes to B and B to A: A and B shoot on goal with a single touch of the ball

SUPPORT PASS AND COORDINATION

18 U11+

 10 Theme : TECHNICAL

EXERCISE

duration   equipment

10

Balls, discs, bars, hoops, cones, bibs (2 colors).

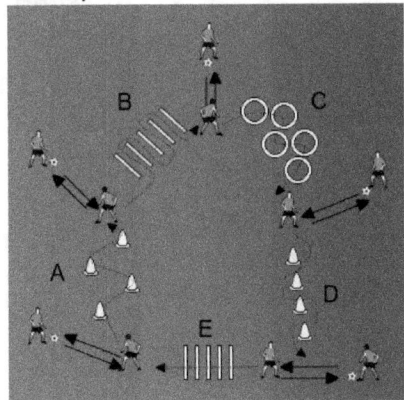

Explanations

Set up coordination stations as shown in the image. Two teams of 5 players.
 The players form a pentagon of 10m on each side.
 The reds have the ball. Red passes to Blue who gives it back to him with a single touch

of the ball. Blue then goes through the coordination station and then receives the pass from the next red player. Switch roles.

Objectives

- Pass
- Support and pass
- Foot work
- Coordination

INSTRUCTIONS

- A : touches the top of each cone
- B : shuffle
- C :1 step per hoop
- D : slalom
- E : 2 quick steps between the bars

VARIATIONS

• Red has the ball in his hands and throws it to Blue who sends it back in one touch

• Pass it back in 2 touches; header; soft touch + pass; etc.

• Change the stations

Dribbling and Passing (2)

19 U7+

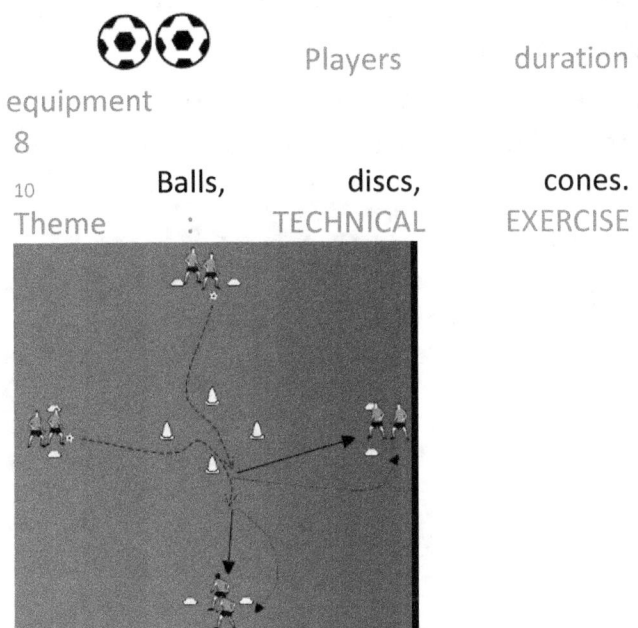

Players   duration

equipment

8

10   **Balls,   discs,   cones.**
Theme   :   TECHNICAL   EXERCISE

Explanations

Two players are placed at each yellow door. These doors are located 10m from the middle area.
 Players with a ball dribble through the middle area and pass to a player without a ball as soon as they leave the area.

Objectives

-   Dribbling
-   Pass
-          Warm-up   routine

INSTRUCTIONS

- The player goes to the line of the player to whom he passed the ball

- Get back in position by doing the warm-up movements (knee up, buttock heels, shuffle, etc.)

VARIATIONS

- Go to the opposite side after the pass
- Play with 3 balls at the same time

First touch and passing exercises

20 **U11+**

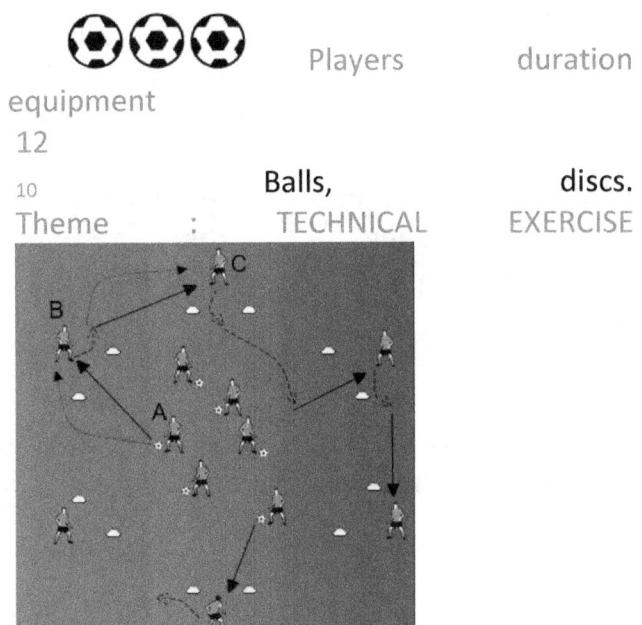

Players   duration

equipment

12

10   **Balls,**   **discs.**

Theme   :   TECHNICAL   EXERCISE

Explanations

6x 2m wide doors are placed on the field be -
hind which a player without a ball is placed.
Players with balls move through the middle
space.
 The player dribbling the ball passes to a
player without a ball through the door.
 The player controls towards another outside

player and passes the ball to him. The latter controls and dribbles his ball into the middle space.

Objectives

- Dribbling
- Pass
- First touch

INSTRUCTIONS

- Take the position of the player to whom you are passing the ball
- The outside players stand 2 m behind the door
- Work with both feet

VARIATIONS

- A passes to B who passes to C who passes to A who asks for the ball again

Ball control (2)

Exercise age difficulty

21 U7+

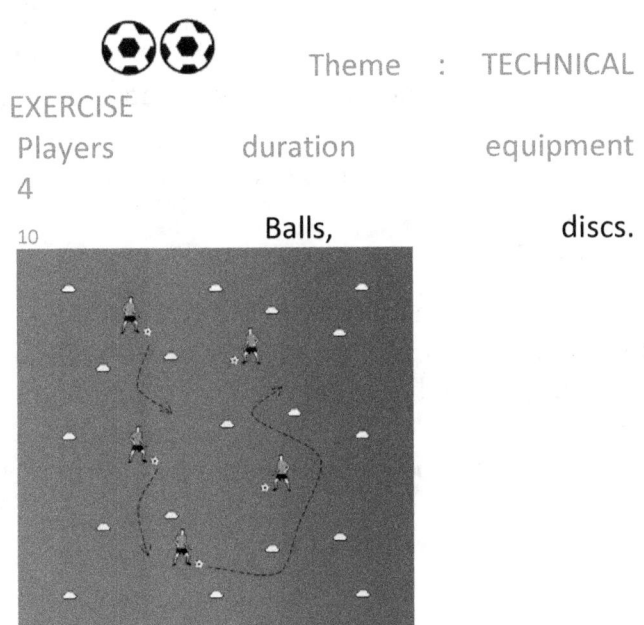

Theme : TECHNICAL EXERCISE

Players   duration   equipment

4

10   Balls,   discs.

Explanations

Surface area of 20x20m with 5x 2m wide doors.
Each player has a ball.
They dribble the ball and follow the coach's instructions.
One point per sequence performed correctly.

Objectives

63

- Dribbling
- 1 vs 1 moves
- Pass

INSTRUCTIONS

- Bypass a disc
- Dribble through doors
- Leave the ball in one door and retrieve another
- Do a 1 vs move 1 in a door to change direction

VARIATIONS

- Stop the ball in a door and do warm-up movements when you collect another ball
- Swap your ball with another player through a door
- Do a nutmeg or kick the ball past another player to beat him

Give and go + defensive stance

Exercise age difficulty

22 **U11+**

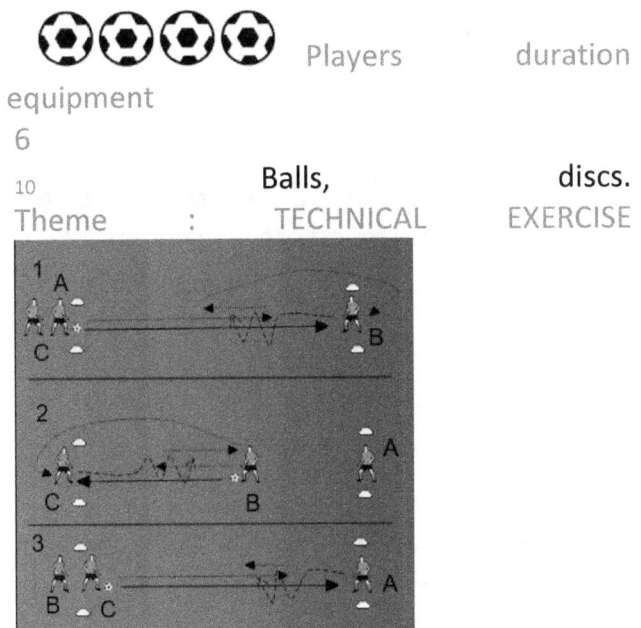

Players   duration

equipment

6

10   **Balls,**   **discs.**

Theme   :   TECHNICAL   EXERCISE

Explanations

Groups of 3 players with a ball for 3. 20m be -
tween discs.

A passes to B then runs towards B with a
proper defensive stance for a few meters
then takes B's place.

While A is in his defensive stance, B makes a
fake and then passes to C. B will then gets in

his defensive stance in front of C. C does a fake, etc.

Objectives

•	Pass
• First	touch
•	Fakes
• Defensive	stance

INSTRUCTIONS
• The image describes the exercise in 3 steps
• Passive defensive stance moving backward without trying to take the ball
• A does a series of fakes without trying to overrun   A
• After a few meters, A continues his run forward and B passes to C

VARIATIONS

• Add a player D behind B: A tries to intercept after being in a defensive stance. If A does not intercept the ball, the exercise carries on. If A intercepts it, then A passes to D and places himself behind D. The exercise continues with D passing to C and defending on C.

Ball control (3)

23 U7-U9

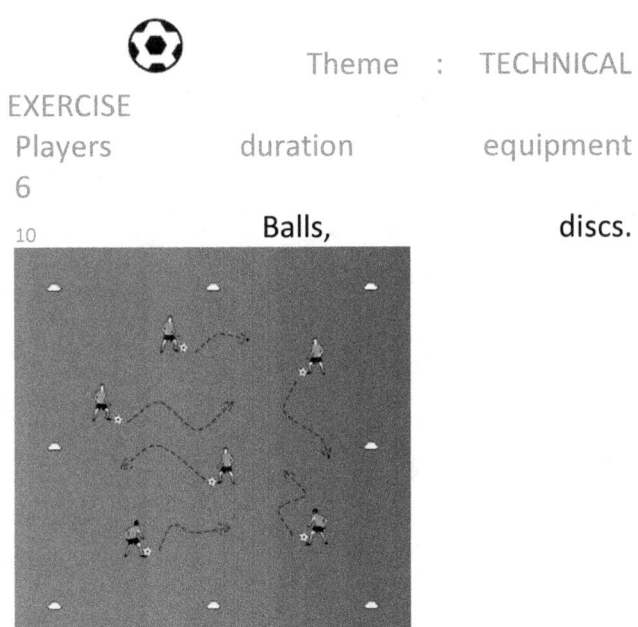

Theme : TECHNICAL
EXERCISE

Players   duration   equipment
6

10   **Balls,**   **discs.**

Explanations

Surface area of 15x15m.
Each player has a ball.
The players dribble the ball. At the whistle, they stop the ball with the body part requested by the coach.

67

INSTRUCTIONS

- Stop with the right foot
- Stop with the left foot
- Stop with the forehead
- Stop the ball by sitting on it
- Stop with the knee

VARIATIONS

- Stop with the back
- Stop with the belly
- Etc.

Objectives

- Dribbling
- Ball control
- Stop the ball

2-MAN TECHNICAL COURSE

Exercise age difficulty Players

24 U11+

 4 Theme : TECHNICAL
EXERCISE

duration   equipment
10

Balls, discs, cones, poles, bars, 1 mi- ni-goal.

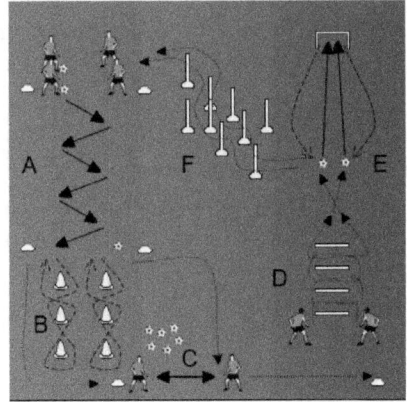

Explanations

Set up the course as described on the image.
Additional balls if necessary. The players
begin the course with a partner. Start at
several
 points along the course to reduce waiting
time.

VARIATIONS

69

- Change partners
- Change stations (passing, dribbling and coordination)
- Time the partners: complete the course as quickly as possible while maintaining technical quality

Objectives

- Dribbling
- Pass
- Foot work
- Coordination

INSTRUCTIONS

- A: One-touch passes

- B: slalom dribbling with a ball each; round trip course then slalom without the ball to go to C

- C: 2-man passing game(one player moves forward, the other goes back), then passes the ball to the ball pile

- D: side steps
- E: shoot on goal and then get the ball back
- F: go through the pole forest to go back to the start

Double give and go

Exercise age difficulty

25 U11+

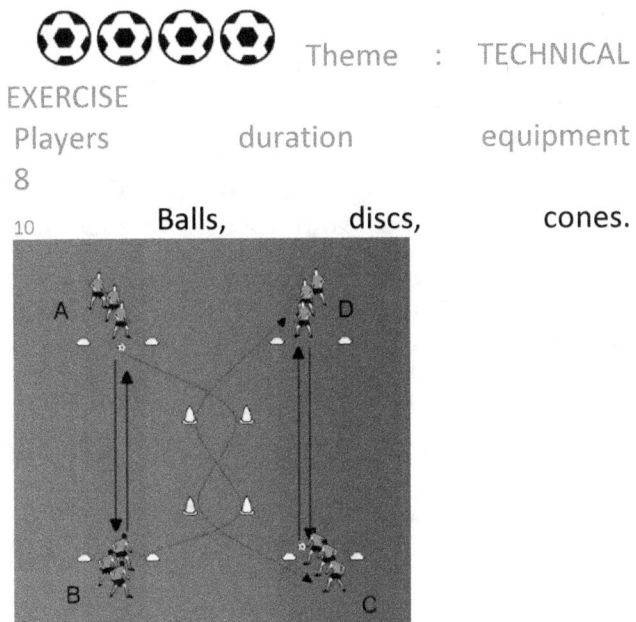 Theme : TECHNICAL EXERCISE

Players   duration   equipment

8

10   **Balls,**   **discs,**   **cones.**

Explanations

Set up the exercise as shown in the picture. 10m between the discs. 6m between the cones of the same color.
 Two "passes and cuts" at the same time: after passing, the player side steps between the cones of the same color and then goes behind the opposite diagonally line.

71

Objectives

-                                     Pass
-         One   touch   play
-           Warm-up   routine

INSTRUCTIONS

- A passes to B then side steps between the yellow cones and goes to C
- At the same time, C passes to D and then side steps between the yellow cones and goes to A
- Always be ready and focus on each pass

VARIATIONS

- Vary the warm up movements to do between the cones

Ball control with areas

26 **U7-U13**

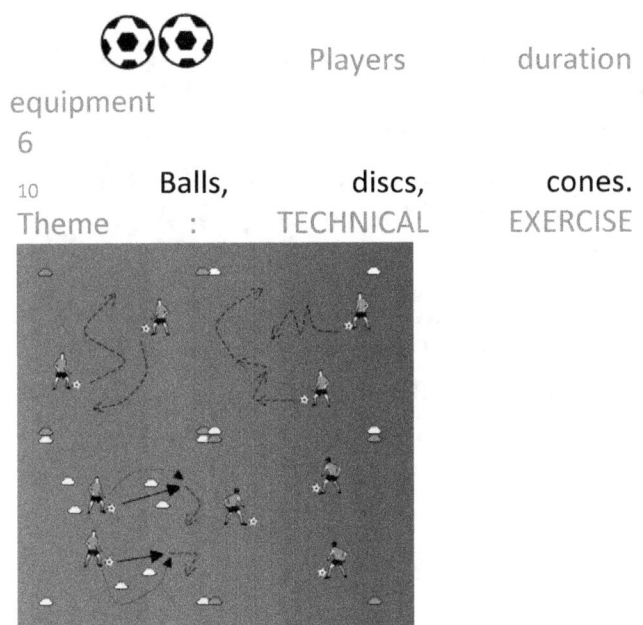

Players   duration

equipment

6

10   **Balls,   discs,   cones.**
Theme   :   TECHNICAL   EXERCISE

Explanations

Surface area of 20x20m divided into 4 areas. The players each dribble a ball and must follow the instructions according to the area in which they are located. They move freely.

Objectives

-                                  Dribbling
-       1   vs   1   moves
- Control of the ball with the different contact surfaces

INSTRUCTIONS

-    Blue   area: fast   dribbling
- White area: a series of dribbles (fakes, hooks, rakes)
- Yellow area: nutmeg on doors and kick the ball past a door to beat it (1m wide)
- Red area: dribble only with the sole

VARIATIONS

- In an area: leave your ball and do the warm-up movements (shuffle, cross steps, etc.)
- In an area: dribble only with the weak foot
- In an area: slalom between the cones

PASSING STATIONS

Exercise age difficulty

27 **U9+**

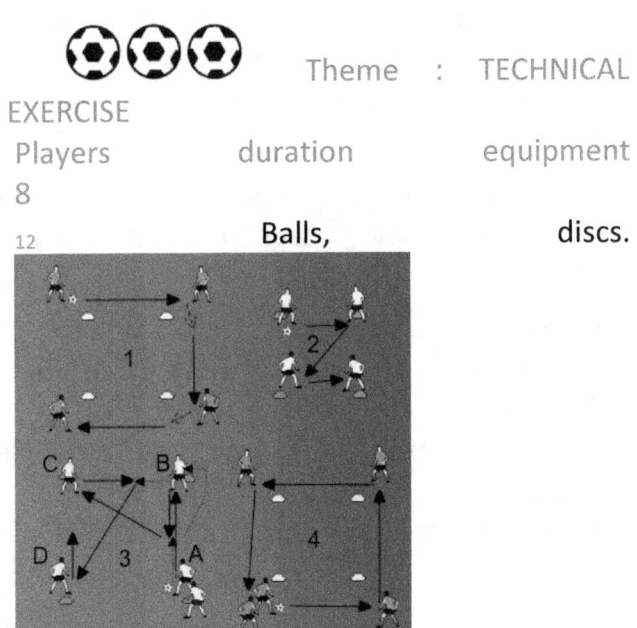

Theme : TECHNICAL EXERCISE

Players   duration   equipment

8

12   Balls,   discs.

Explanations

Set up several pass stations.
Groups of 4 or 5 players per station.
Each group plays for 3 minutes at a station and then goes to the next.

Objectives

75

-   Pass
-          One   touch   play
- First   touch   +   pass   sequence

INSTRUCTIONS

- 1: control + pass to the next player. Everything is done outside the 6x6m square
- 2: free passes without control inside the 5x5m square

- 3: A passes to B who passes to A. A passes to C. C passes to B who passes to D. Move after the pass

- 4: passes with a single touch of the ball outside the 6x6m square. Follow your pass

VARIATIONS

- Do the same exercises in groups of 3 (triangle formation)
- Let the players know which foot to work with

TECHNICAL COURSE

28 U9+

 8 Theme : TECHNICAL

EXERCISE

duration   equipment

10

Balls, discs, poles, hoops, cones, 1 mini-goal.

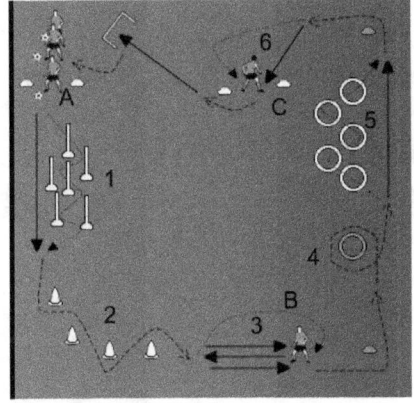

Explanations

Set up the course as shown in the image.
1: pass to yourself and then cross the forest of poles
2: enter the slalom when A finishes the slalom 3: double support pass and take B's spot
4: B dribbles around the hoop

5: B passes to himself and makes 1 step per hoop

6: B passes to C who controls and shoots on goal. B takes C's spot. C goes to the starting position.

Objectives

- Dribbling
- Pass
- Foot work

INSTRUCTIONS

- Keep control of the ball
- The next player starts the course

VARIATIONS

- Change the coordination stations: coordination latter, side steps between bars, etc.
- Add other stations to extend the course and reduce waiting time

TECHNICAL sequence

Exercise age difficulty

29 U11+

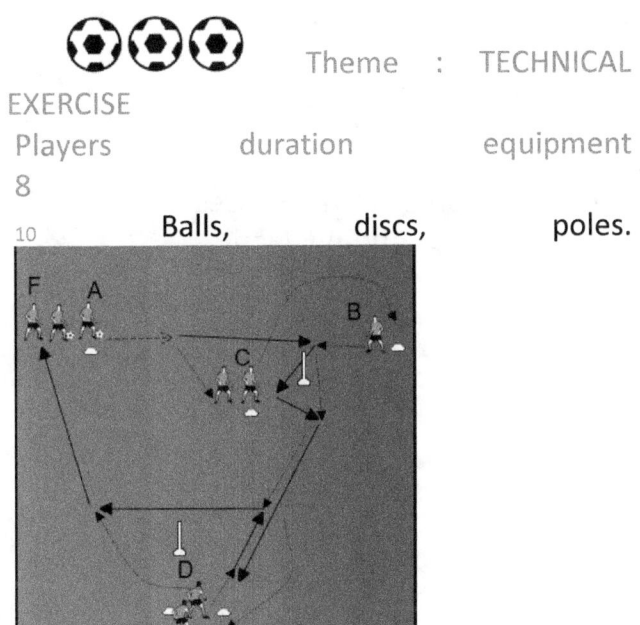

Theme : TECHNICAL EXERCISE

Players	duration	equipment
8	10	Balls, discs, poles.

Explanations

Players position themselves as shown in the picture. A, B and C form a triangle of 16m on each side.

A dribbles the ball and passes to B who runs deep. B does a one-two with C and then gives to D who's running deep. B passes in-stride to D who calls for a through ball. D passes to F.

79

Objectives

- Dribbling
- Pass
- One-two
- Lead pass

INSTRUCTIONS

- After his pass, A goes to C; C to B; B to D; D to F
- Focus on doing quality passes
- Check before running deep

VARIATIONS

- D ends with a shot on goal

coordination course

30 U7+

 Theme : TECHNICAL EXERCISE

Players	duration	equipment
6		10

Discs, hoops, bars, cones, bibs (2 colors).

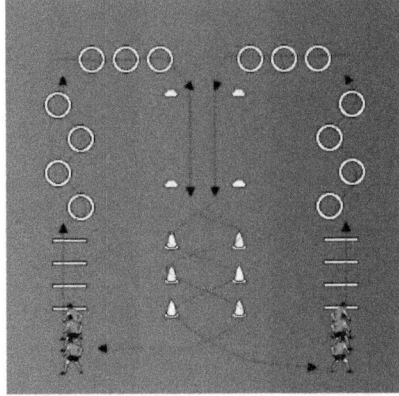

Explanations

Set up 2 identical coordination courses next to each other.

Players complete the course several times.

When a player finishes the course, the next one starts.

Objectives

- Foot work

81

- Coordination

INSTRUCTIONS

- 2 quick steps between the bars
- 1 step in each white hoop
- Joined feet step in the yellow hoops
- Reverse running between the white discs
- Shuffle from one cone to another before going back to position

VARIATIONS

- Duels: 1 blue and 1 red start at the whistle. The first one to finish wins
- Add a 3rd course if there are more than 12 players
- Vary the coordination stations

TECHNICAL AND COORDINATION COURSE

Exercise age difficulty

31 U9+

 Players   duration

equipment

6

10 Balls, discs, cones, bars, bibs (2 colors).
Theme   :   TECHNICAL   EXERCISE

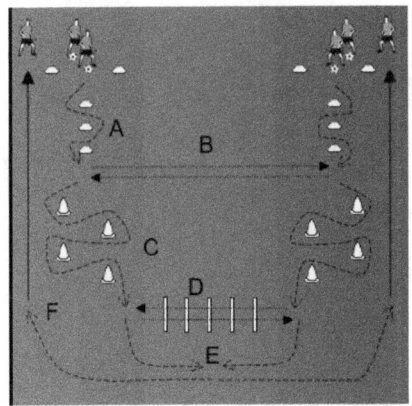

Explanations

Set up two identical courses as shown in the image.
 One player from each team starts at the same time.
 The next two players start when the first play- ers arrive at station B.

Objectives

- Dribbling
- Foot work
- Coordination
- Pass

INSTRUCTIONS
- A : slalom between the discs and then stop the ball
- B : shuffle to the other side
- C : retrieve the ball and slalom between the cones and then leave the ball there
- D : 2 quick steps between the bars and recover the ball
- E : screen with the other player
- F : dribble and pass to the player waiting then get back to the start

VARIATIONS
- Vary the dribbling and coordination stations
- Add 2 courses if there are too many players to reduce the waiting time

DRIBBLING AND PASSing EXERCISE

Exercise age difficulty

32 U11+

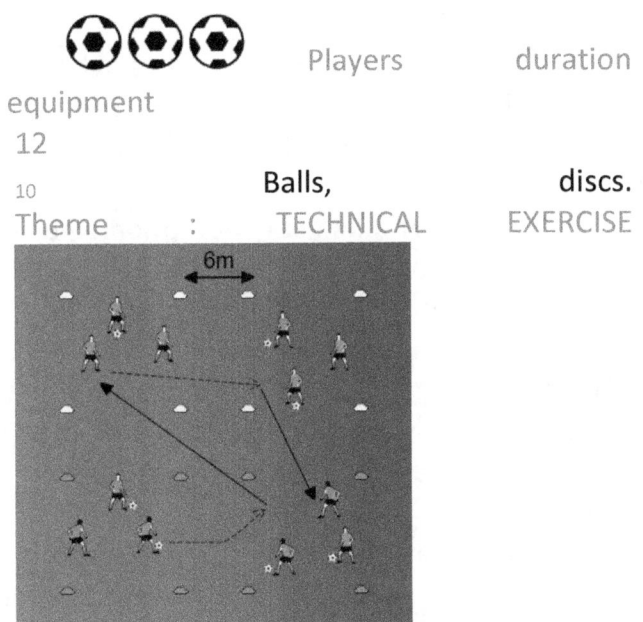

Players   duration

equipment

12

10   Balls,   discs.

Theme   :   TECHNICAL   EXERCISE

Explanations

Set up 4 squares of 8x8m of different colors.
12 players are divided into these squares with
7 balls in play.
A player who has a ball must dribble it into a square before passing to a free player from another square.

Objectives

-   Dribbling
-   Pass
-   Information gathering

INSTRUCTIONS

• The player who has or receives a ball changes square before he can pass his ball
• Gather information to know who to pass to and when
• Players without a ball stay in motion to offer passing solutions to the ball carriers
• A player without a ball must stay in his square

VARIATIONS

• Passes are only allowed between yellow and blue squares, and between white and red squares
• Passes are only allowed between yellow and red squares, and between white and blue squares

TWO-MAN JUGGLING

Exercise age difficulty

33 U11+

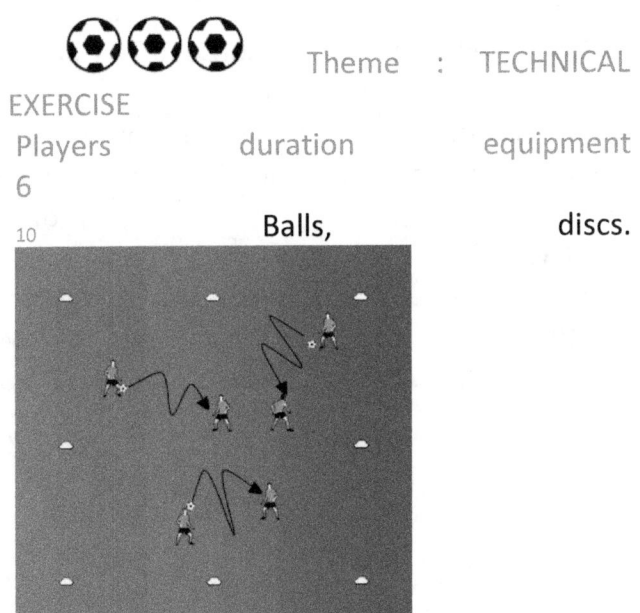

Theme : TECHNICAL EXERCISE

Players   duration   equipment

6

10   Balls,   discs.

Explanations

20x20m playing surface.
Groups of 2 with 1 ball. Players pass the ball around, letting the ball bounce once before passing it. The team that makes the most consecutive passes without errors wins.

Objectives

- Finesse ball touch
- Juggling
- Control of a lifted pass

INSTRUCTIONS
- A single touch of the ball
- Count the number of consecutive passes made without error
- Start counting again in the event of an error
- Players can move around the field to avoid other groups

VARIATIONS
- Same game in groups of 3 players
- Same game but you can juggle before passing: 5 juggles maximum before a pass

JUGGLING RELAYS

Exercise age difficulty

34 **U11+**

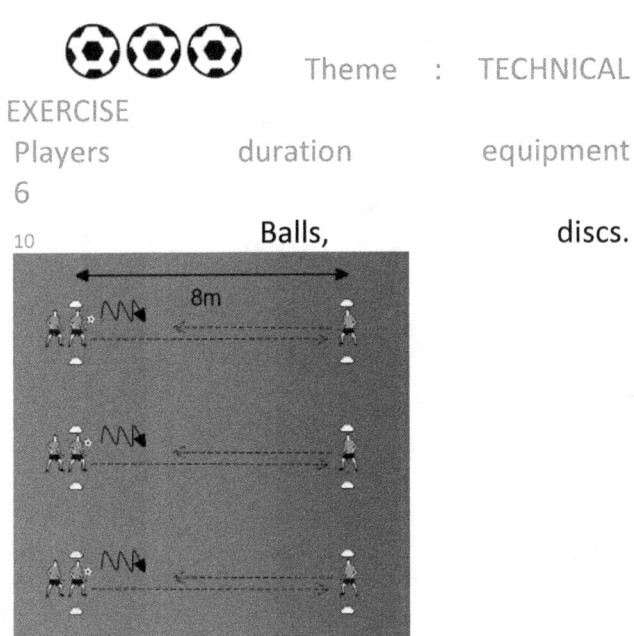

Theme : TECHNICAL EXERCISE

Players   duration   equipment

6

10   **Balls,**   discs.

Explanations

Groups of 3 players with one ball for 3.
At the whistle, A juggles to B and passes to B.
B juggles to C and passes to C. C juggles to A,
the player takes the spot of his partner after
passing to him (A stays in B; B stays in C; etc.)
The team that does the most back and forth

without dropping the ball in a given time wins.

VARIATIONS

• Add obstacles to avoid (cones, hurdles, poles)
• Reduce the distance (4m): A passes in the air to B then runs in B; B juggles and passes in the air to C then runs in C; etc.

Objectives

•   Juggling
•   Controlling a ball in the air
•   Improve   ball   touch
•   Balance and coordination

INSTRUCTIONS

• Count the number of back and forth without errors in 2 minutes
• If the ball falls, start from 0 again and keep the best score

JUGGLING DUEL

Exercise age difficulty

35 **U9-U15**

Theme : TECHNICAL

EXERCISE

Players   duration   equipment
12
10   Balls,   discs.

Explanations

Set up 6 playing fields of 5x5m.
Number the fields from 1 to 6.
Two players per square with a ball each.
Make the maximum number of juggles in a
row in 1'30". If the ball falls, start counting

from 0 again, keep the best score to determine who wins.

Objectives

- Control of a lifted pass
- Juggling
- Improve ball touch

INSTRUCTIONS

- The winner moves up a field (towards field 1)
- The loser goes down a field (towards field 6)
- Quick draw in case of a tie
- At the end of the game, the winners are those who are on field number 1

VARIATIONS

- Define the type of juggling: strong foot, weak foot, head, alternate right foot, left foot, etc.
- Same for teams of 2 players: count the number of exchanges

THE TRAIN GAME

Exercise age difficulty

36 **U7-U13**

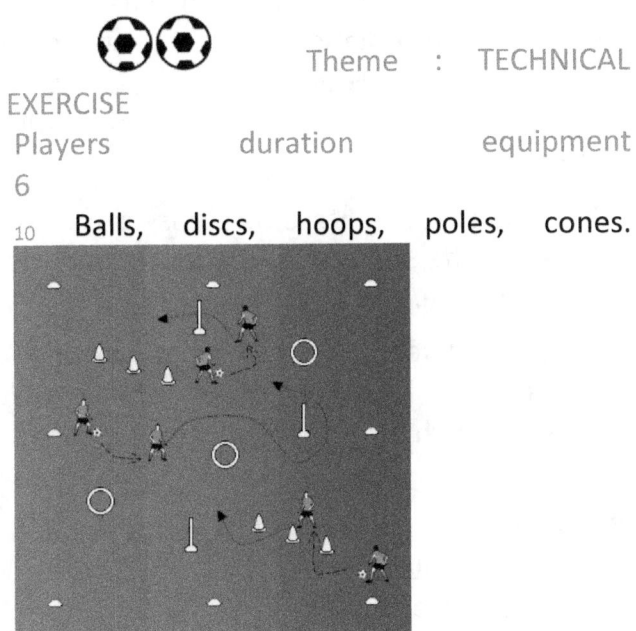

⚽⚽   Theme   :   TECHNICAL
EXERCISE
Players   duration   equipment
6
10   **Balls,   discs,   hoops,   poles,   cones.**

Explanations

20x20m field with hoops, cones (sla -
lom-shaped) and scattered poles. In groups
of
2 players with one ball for 2.
Red moves around the field without a ball
and do warm-up movements while going to

the small stations encountered on his way. Blue follows him by dribbling the ball.

Objectives

- Dribbling
- Control of a moving ball
- Information gathering
- Foot work
- Coordination

INSTRUCTIONS

• Warm-up movements: side steps, crossed steps, knee lifts, heels to buttocks, defender's steps, back race, etc.

• Slalom between the cones; go around a hoop, do a fake in front of a pole
• Switch roles regularly

VARIATIONS

• Same with 3 players: one locomotive and 2 wagons with balls
• Vary the obstacles
• Speed change announced by the coach

8 VS 3 BALL possession

Exercise age difficulty

37 U11+

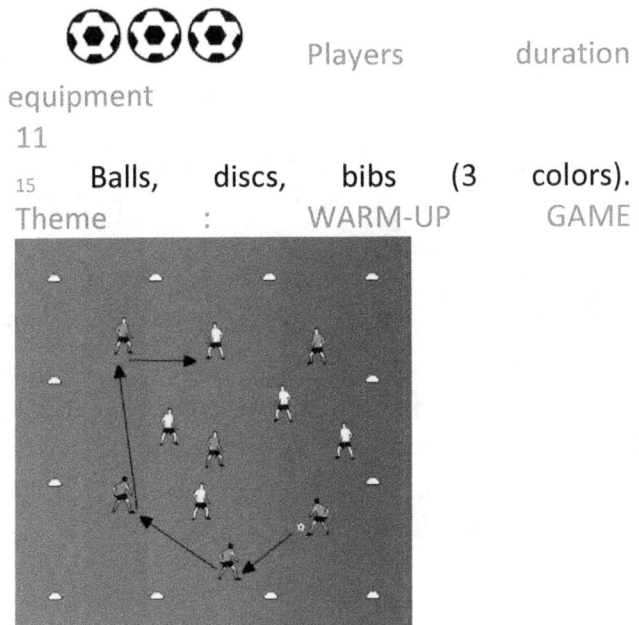

Players   duration
equipment
11
15   Balls,   discs,   bibs   (3   colors).
Theme   :   WARM-UP   GAME

Explanations

Surface area of 35x25m. Three teams of 3 play - ers + 2 jokers.
 Two teams try to keep the ball against a third team that tries to recover it.
 The team that loses the ball has to defend. Blues and reds play against the yellows with the help of 2 white jokers.

95

VARIATIONS

• Limit the number of ball touches
• Add 2 mini-goals: teams in possession of the ball that have made 10 consecutive passes without los- ing the ball can try to score in one of the 2 goals

Objectives

• Support to the ball carrier
• Information gathering
• First touch + pass sequence

INSTRUCTIONS

• The 2 jokers always play with the teams in possession of the ball
• If a joker loses the ball, the coach chooses and announces the next defending team
• Offer passing solutions to the ball carrier
• Look for and create space

ONE-TOUCH BALL possession

Exercise age difficulty

38 **U13+**

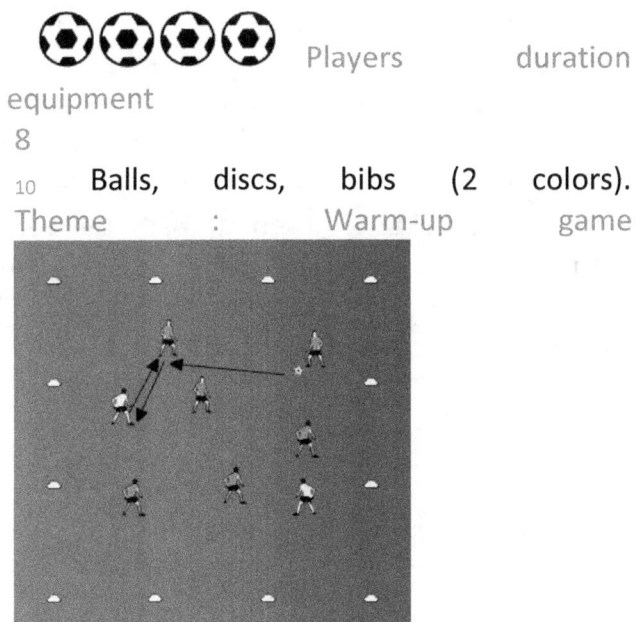

Players   duration   equipment

8

10   **Balls,   discs,   bibs   (2   colors).**
Theme   :   Warm-up   game

Explanations

Surface area of 20x20m. Two teams of 3 play
- ers + 2 jokers.
 Players are limited to 1 ball touch. Make the
most passes without losing possession of the
ball.
 The jokers always play with the team in possession of the ball.

97

Objectives

- Support the ball carrier
- Information gathering
- One touch play

INSTRUCTIONS
- Always be in motion to offer solutions
- Focus on quality passes
- Gather information

VARIATIONS
- Pass to a joker = 1 point, pass between partners = 2 points
- Add 2 mini-goals: try to score in one of the 2 goals after 6 consecutive passes

THIEVES' GAME

39 **U7-U11**

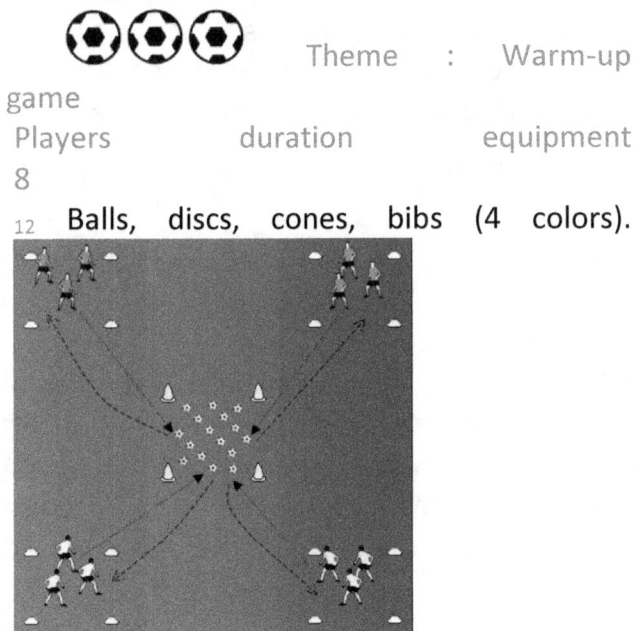

Theme : Warm-up game

Players duration equipment
8
12 **Balls, discs, cones, bibs (4 colors).**

Explanations

Set up the game as shown in the picture. The houses are located 10m from the area with the balls.

At the whistle, the players will retrieve the balls and dribble them back. When there are

99

no more balls in the middle, go steal some from other houses.

VARIATIONS

• Pass to your partner from the middle area
• The coach scatters discs in the middle area when there are no more balls in the middle: players must avoid the discs. A player who touches a disc must bring the ball back to the house where he stole it and take another one

Objectives

•   Dribbling
•   Passing

INSTRUCTIONS

• Player must go through the middle area on the way forth and back
• Do not defend: let the opponent take the balls in the house
• Take one ball at a time

THE MOVERS

40 U7-U11

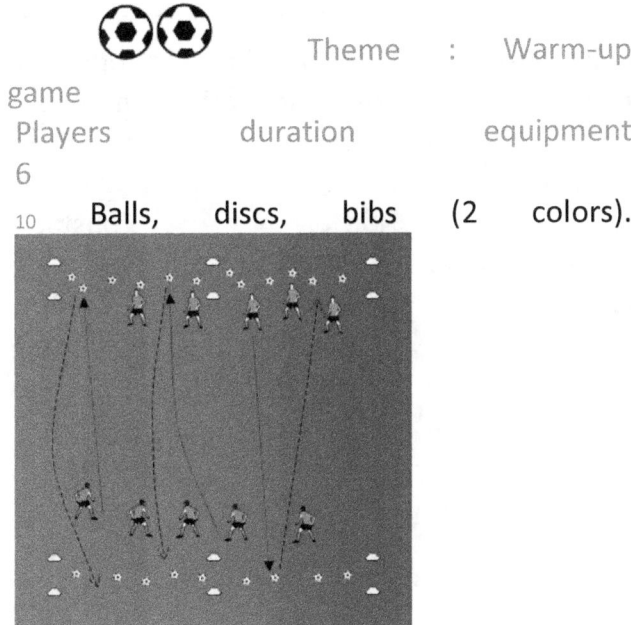

Theme : Warm-up game

Players   duration   equipment

6

10   **Balls,   discs,   bibs   (2   colors).**

Explanations

Set up two 15x3m areas 15m away from each other.

A team is in front of each area.

At the whistle, blues and reds will retrieve the balls from the opposing area and dribble them back to their area.

Objectives

- Dribbling
- Speed
- Information gathering

INSTRUCTIONS

- Take one ball at a time
- Be careful not to run into an opponent
- After 3 minutes: the team with the most balls wins

VARIATIONS

- Add obstacles
- Add coordination stations to be done before taking a ball

4 AGAINST 4 WITH ZONES

Exercise age difficulty

41 U13+

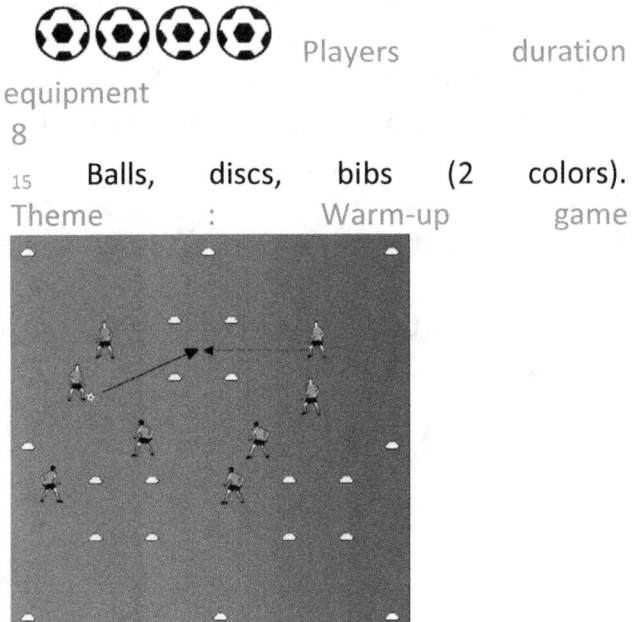

Players   duration
equipment
8
15   Balls,   discs,   bibs   (2   colors).
Theme   :   Warm-up   game

Explanations

25x25m square with 3 separate 2.5x2.5m are
- as inside.
4 vs 4 game. To score, a player must receive a
pass from a partner in one of the 3 areas.

Objectives

- Passing
- Lead pass
- Offer passing solutions to the ball carrier

INSTRUCTIONS
- The player must control the ball in the area for the point to count
- The game continues after a point is scored
- Players can move freely on the entire field
- Players can defend in the areas

VARIATIONS
- The ball must arrive in the area before the player (lead pass)
- Score a point by passing to a partner through one of the areas

3 versus 1 keep-away

Exercise age difficulty Players

42 U13+

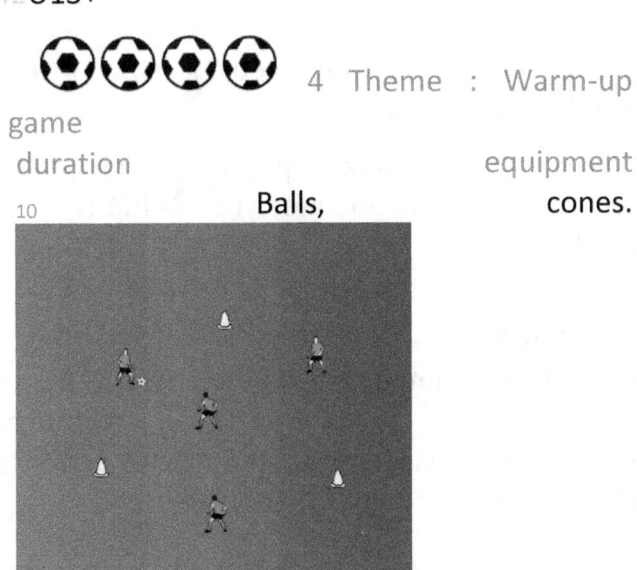 4 Theme : Warm-up
game
duration   equipment
10   Balls,   cones.

Explanations

Groups of 4 players with one ball for 4. Blues try to keep the ball against reds.
Each blue must stay on their side of the triangle. The player who loses their ball becomes a de- fender.

Objectives

- Support the ball carrier
- Offer passing solutions
- Precise and dosed passes
- Reduce pass angles

INSTRUCTIONS
- If a defender is nutmeged, he stays in the middle one more round

- If the attackers make 6 passes in a row, the defender remains one more round in the middle

- Free play

VARIATIONS
- Limit the number of ball touches (3, 2 and then 1 touch)
- Reduce the size of the triangle to increase intensity and difficulty for attackers

6 VS 6 GAME WITH TARGETS

Exercise age difficulty

43 U11+

⚽⚽⚽   Players   duration

equipment

12

15   **Balls, discs, bibs (2 colors).**
Theme   :   Warm-up   game

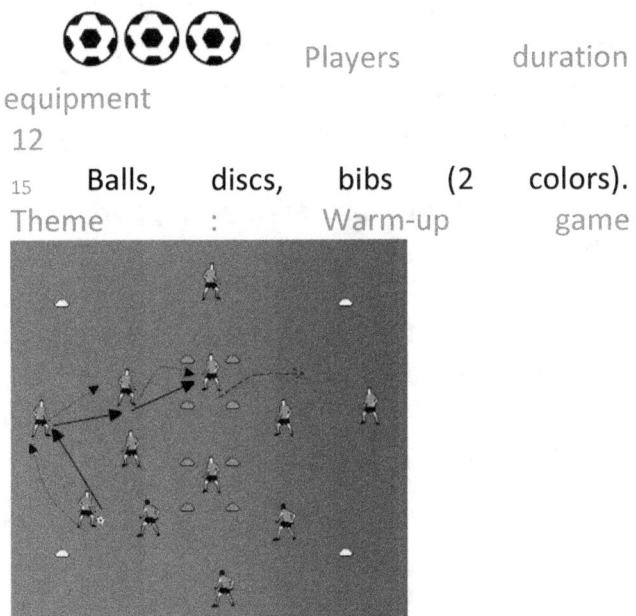

Explanations

25x25m square with 2 separate 2.5x2.5m are
- as in the middle of the square.
One player from each team in the inner
squares. 2 support players on the sides.
To score, pass the ball to the target player of
his team.

Objectives

107

- Support the ball carrier
- Offer passing solutions
- Focus on quality passes

INSTRUCTIONS

- The point counts if the target player controls the received ball
- Only targets can be in the middle areas
- The player who passes to the target player takes his place
- The player who passes to a support player takes his place

VARIATIONS

- No fixed target: a player can become a target for 5 seconds and then must leave the area
- The target players have no color: you can score on both targets

GAME OF COLORS

Exercise age difficulty

44 **U7-U11**

Theme : Warm-up game

Players duration equipment

4

10 Balls, discs.

Explanations

Surface area of 15x15m. Spread different colored discs on the field. Players move around the field and follow the coach's instruc- tions.

Objectives

- Foot work
- Coordination
- Speed

INSTRUCTIONS
- Touch the requested color disc
- Touch 3 different colored discs in the requested order
- Run fast and avoid the discs
- Pick up a disc and drop it off at another place

VARIATIONS
- Same game but players must hold hands with a partner
- Same game with players must dribble ball

HUNTER'S GAME

Exercise age difficulty

45 U9+

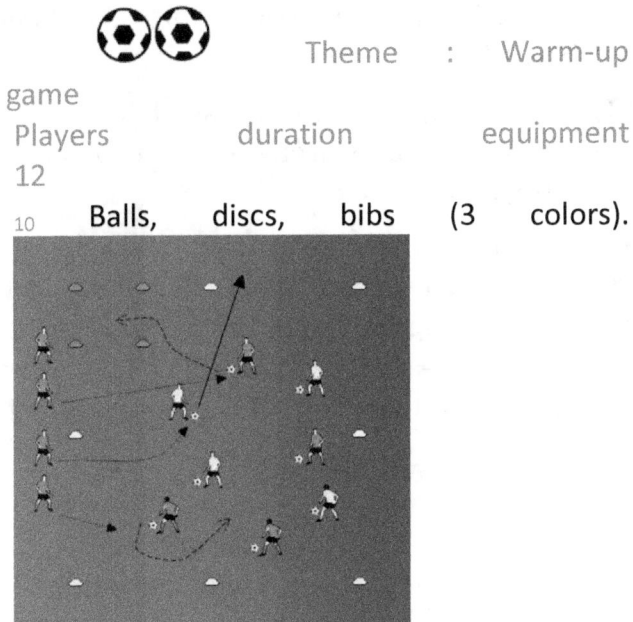

Theme : Warm-up game

Players duration equipment

12

10 Balls, discs, bibs (3 colors).

Explanations

20x20m square with a 3x3m blue square in one of the corners of the bigger square.
The reds and yellows each have a ball and drib- ble it into the field.
The four blues are on the outside. At the whis- tle, the blues try to get all the balls out of the playing area.

Objectives

-   Dribbling
-                 1   vs   1
-               Ball   protection
- Maintaining   possession   of   the   ball

INSTRUCTIONS

• The blues score 1 point for each ball brought into the blue area before the ball is out of the field

• A yellow player who lost his ball helps his partners keep possession of the balls
• The game stops when all the balls are out or in the blue area
• Switch roles: the team with the most points wins

VARIATIONS

• The yellows help the yellows and the reds help the reds: the last team with the ball before blue takes it out scores 1 point
• Replace the blue area with 2 mini-goals in opposite corners

4 VS 4 GAME

46 U9+

Theme : Small sided games

Players   duration   equipment

8

15 Balls, discs, cones, bibs (2 colors).

Explanations

Surface area of 20x20m with 4 cones scattered on the field.
 Play 4 vs 4. Knock down the cones by shooting them to score.

Objectives

- Reduced number of players
- Reduced surface area

INSTRUCTIONS

- 1 point for a yellow cone
- 3 points for a white cone
- The game continues even when a cone is knocked down (the coach puts it back in place)

VARIATIONS

- Knocking down a cone with a single touch of the ball counts double
- Add 1 or 2 offensive jokers
- 3 red cones and 3 blue cones: attack the opponents' cones

4 VS 4 TRIANGLE GAME

Exercise age difficulty Players

47 **U11+**

 8 Theme : Small sided games

duration   equipment

15 **Balls, discs, 3 poles, bibs (2 colors).**

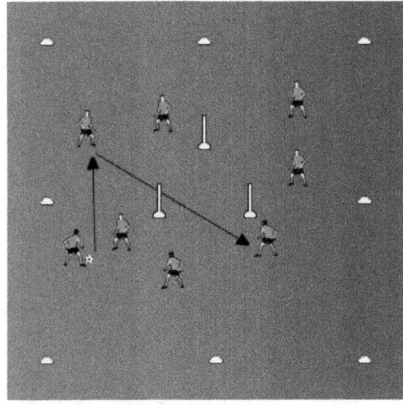

Explanations

Surface area of 25x25m. 3 poles form a 3m wide triangle in the middle of the square.
Play 4 against 4. To score, pass the ball to a partner through one of the 3 sides of the trian- gle.

Objectives

- Reduced number of players
- Reduced surface area

INSTRUCTIONS

- One point per pass through the triangle
- The point only counts if the partner manages to control the ball
- Play continues after a point is scored: the team retains possession of the ball

VARIATIONS

- A successful support pass through the same side gives 3 points (one-touch passing)
- A successful 3-player passing sequence through 2 different sides scores 5 points (one touch pass from the 2nd player to the 3rd)
- Adapt the size of the field and triangle to your players

4 VS 4 MATCH WITH MODULAR TEAMS

48 **U9+**

 8 Theme : Small sided games

duration   equipment

15 **Balls, discs, mini-goals, bibs (4 colors).**

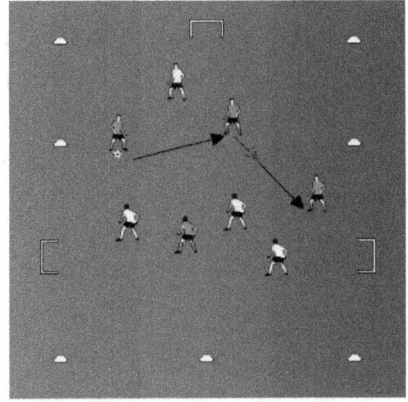

Explanations

35x20m surface area with 3 mini-goals.
4 teams of 2 players.
Play 4 vs 4: during the game, the coach in-
structs which teams are playing together.
Here, the blues and reds play against the
yellows and whites.

VARIATIONS

- Play with 2 mini-goals
- Add doors through which players have to dribble the ball to score
- Play with 2 goals with goalkeepers

Objectives

- Reduced number of players
- Reduced surface area

INSTRUCTIONS

- Players can score on all 3 goals
- The coach can change the teams that play together at any time
- Regular changes: for example, yellow and blue against white and red
- Players must adapt quickly

5 VS 5 GAMES WITH TARGETS

Exercise age difficulty Players

49 U7+

10 Theme : Small sided games
duration   equipment
15 Balls, discs, cones, bibs (2 colors).

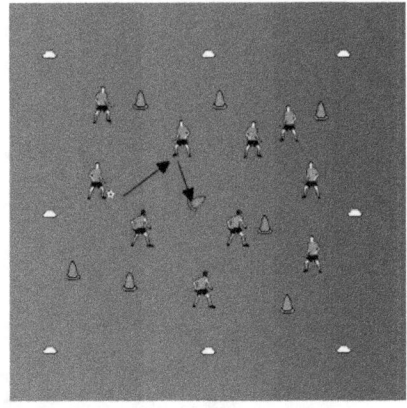

Explanations

Surface area of 25x25m. Disperse 4 blue cones and 4 red cones.
5 vs 5 game. To score, knock down the oppos- ing team's cones by shooting at them with the ball.

Objectives

- Reduced number of players
- Reduced surface area

INSTRUCTIONS
- Put the ball back into play by dribbling or passing it
- It is forbidden to touch the cones with your feet

VARIATIONS

- A cone knocked down by the weak foot counts double
- Players can knock down all the cones (reds and blues)
- Adapt the size of the field and the number of targets according to the age/level of the players

Match 4 versus 4 with mini-goals

Exercise age difficulty Players

50 U7+

 8 Theme : Small sided games

duration   equipment

15 Balls, discs, bibs (2 colors), 2 mini-goals.

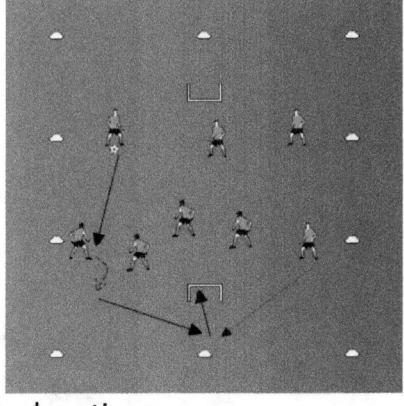

Explanations

35x20m field with mini-goals inside facing back to the flow of the game.
 Players cannot shoot from far away and must progress forward to score.

Objectives

• Reduced number of players

121

- Reduced surface area

INSTRUCTIONS

- No throw-ins: put the ball back into play by dribbling or passing it
- Free play

VARIATIONS

- Play 3 vs 3
- Use 4 mini-goals
- Limit the number of ball touches

3 vs 3 game

EXERCISE Age difficultY

51U9+

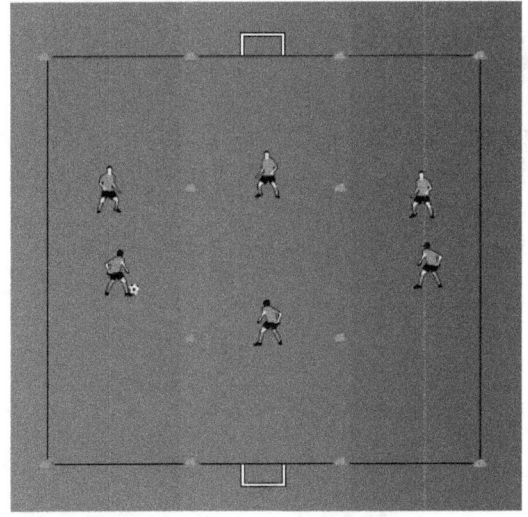

Theme : Small sided games

Players	Duration	EQUIPMENT
6	15	Balls, discs, mini-goals, bibs (2 colors).

Explanations

30x20 meter field with small goals (2 meters). Field split in 3 zones vertically. One player of each team in each zone. Each

player has to stay in his or her zone.
3 vs 3 game.

Objectives

•   Reduced   number   of   players
•   Reduced   surface   area

INSTRUCTIONS

• Playing several rounds : players change zone at   each   round
• Players support teammates as much as possible   staying   in   their   area
•   Everyone   can   score

VARIATIONS

• A player who dribbles an opponent may change area (and return to his area as soon as the ball is lost)
• Only the player in the middle zone can score

Dribbling + pass

52 **U9+**

6 Theme : Warm up -
TECHNICAL   EXERCISE
Duration   EQUIPMENT
12   **Balls,**   **discs.**

Explanations

Groups of six or more/two balls. Players form a circle approximately 12 m in diameter. One or two players have a ball.
A player who has a ball dribbles it for a few meters and passes it to a teammate without a

ball. He then takes the teammate's place and his teammate continues the exercise (dribbling and passing).

Objectives

- Dribbling
- Information gathering
- First touch
- Pass

INSTRUCTIONS
- Dribbling + passing sequence
- Attack the ball
- Pay attention not to pass the ball to the same player

VARIATIONS
- Ask players to make a fake before passing
- 2 touches (First touch + Pass)

First touch + Pass

53 U11+

⚽⚽⚽

8 Theme : Warm up -
TECHNICAL EXERCISE
Duration EQUIPMENT
12 Balls, discs.

Explanations

All the players are inside an area of 20x25 me
- ters. One ball for 2 players.
Players move and pass the ball to each other.
Groups consist of 2 players.
After a few minutes, set the following rule:

everybody plays together (no more groups); it's forbidden to pass the ball to the player who just passed you the ball.

Objectives

- First   touch
- Pass
- Facing   the   play
- Asking   for   the   ball

INSTRUCTIONS
- After a pass, go wide and face the play
- Ask the ball in your feet
- Information   gathering
- Offer passing options to the ball carrier

VARIATIONS
- Call the name of the player you want to pass the ball to (communication)
- Try to pass to a different player every time (then do it again once you play to all the players)

Dribbling keeping the head up

54U7+

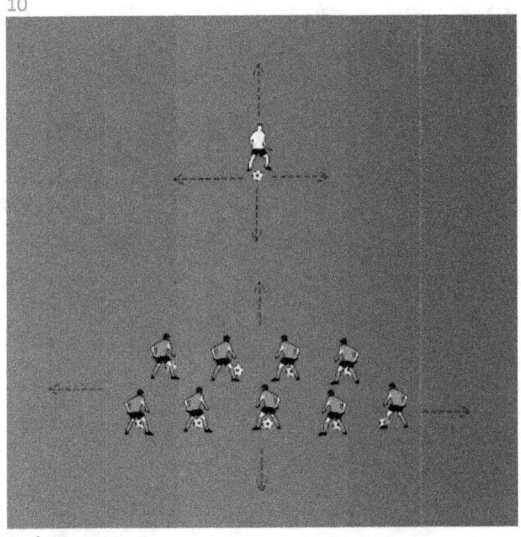

6 Theme : Warm up -
TECHNICAL   EXERCISE
Duration   EQUIPMENT
10   **Balls.**

Explanations

The players form two or three lines. The train
- er has a ball and faces all the player.
 The trainer dribbles the ball, changing direction regularly and using different parts of the
foot. The players try to imitate the trainer by

129

dribbling in the same direction and using the same part of the foot as the trainer.

Objectives

- Dribbling
- Use the different contact surfaces
- Information gathering

INSTRUCTIONS

- Observe moves from the coach
- Keep an eye on the ball
- Keep the ball near you

VARIATIONS

- Dribbling the ball forward, backward, sideward, diagonally, quickly, slowly, with the sole, using inside, outside, etc.

Ball hunter

EXERCISE Age

55 U6-U15

difficultY   Players   Duration   EQUIPMENT

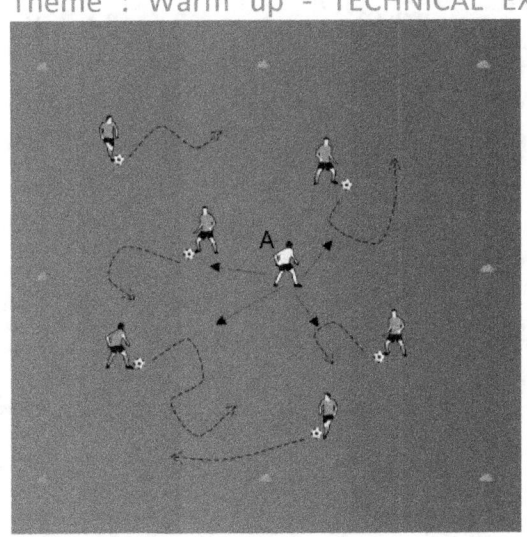

5

10   Balls,   discs.

Theme : Warm up - TECHNICAL EXERCISE

Explanations

Field is 20x20 sq. m. All the players are inside the field. Each player has a ball except the defender 'A'.
'A' tries to kick the ball out of the field. When

131

a player loses the ball he becomes a defender like 'A'.

The winner is the last player who still has his ball.

Do several rounds.

Objectives

- Dribbling
- 1 vs 1 moves
- Looking for free space
- Information gathering

INSTRUCTIONS
- Players must always be moving
- Keep the ball near you
- Play where there are less defenders
- Protect your ball

VARIATIONS
- Dicrease or increase the size of the field
- Start with 2 defenders for younger children

Dribbling keeping the head up (2)

56 U6-U15

5 Theme : Warm up -

TECHNICAL EXERCISE

Duration EQUIPMENT

10 Balls, discs.

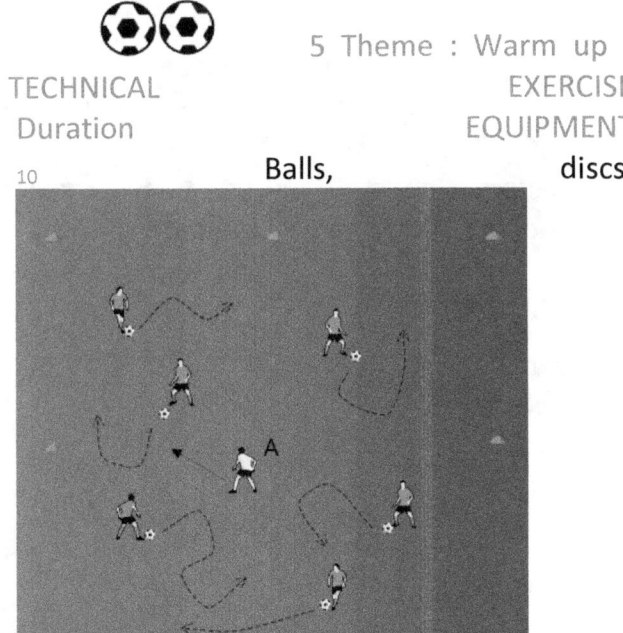

Explanations

Field is 20x20 sq. m. All the players are inside the field. Each player has a ball except the defender 'A'.

'A' tries to take a ball from one of the

133

attackers. When he is successful he becomes an attacker and the attacker takes his place and becomes the new defender.

Objectives

- Dribbling
- 1 vs 1 moves
- Looking for free space
- Information gathering

INSTRUCTIONS

- Players must always be moving
- The defender tries to get the ball back (not to kick it away)

VARIATIONS

- 2 defenders
- 3 defenders
- 4 defenders

Dribbling keeping the head up (3)

57 U11+

⚽⚽⚽   12 Theme : Warm up -
TECHNICAL   EXERCISE
Duration   EQUIPMENT
12   **Balls,   cones,   bibs   (1   color).**

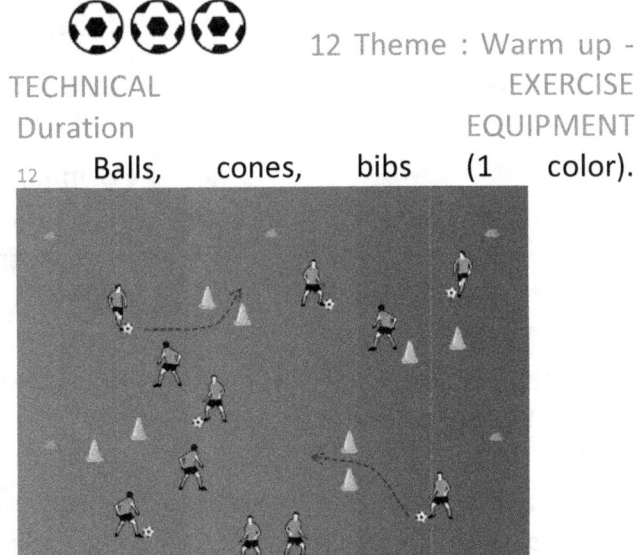

Explanations

8 attackers/4 defenders/8 balls.
Using cones, form small goals (2 m.) that you will spread out on the field (25x25 sq. m.). The eight attackers each have a ball and the four defenders do not. To score, the attackers

135

have to dribble the ball past the defenders and
 through one of the small goals.
 One point is given for each goal.
 The winner is the player who scores the most goals within 1 1/2 minutes. Do several rounds, changing the defenders each time.

Objectives

- Dribbling
- Protect your ball
- Play in free spaces
- Information gathering

INSTRUCTIONS

- Keep the ball near your feet
- Dribbling keeping the head up

VARIATIONS

• No color : when a player loses the ball he becomes a defender
• Set up goals of different colors : scoring in a blue goal gives 2 points ; in a yellow 3 points ; etc.

1-2

58U11+

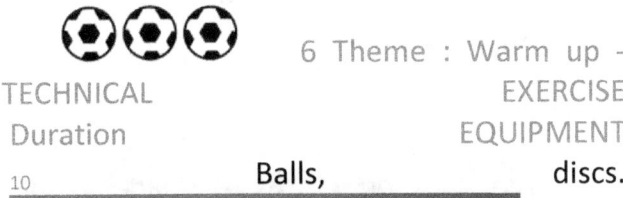

6 Theme : Warm up -
TECHNICAL   EXERCISE
Duration   EQUIPMENT
10   **Balls,**   discs.

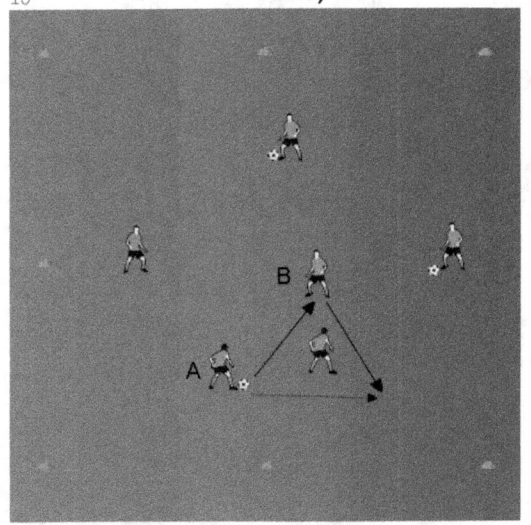

Explanations

All the players are inside a 30x30 square meter area. Groups of 2 players and one ball per group.
The objective is to make 1-2. To make a valua- ble 1-2, player must pass to his

teammate and receive a lead pass after having run behind another player. 1 point per good 1-2.

Example : A and B play together. A passes to B ; B passes back to A (one touch) who gets the ball back after going around the defender.

Objectives

- One-two
- Ask for a lead pass
- Asking for the ball

INSTRUCTIONS
- All the players must be moving
- Pass and sprint to ask for a 1-2
- Accurate passes

VARIATIONS
- Form 2 teams : payers of a same team can play together and try to make 1-2 against players from the other team

1-2 (2)

59 U13+

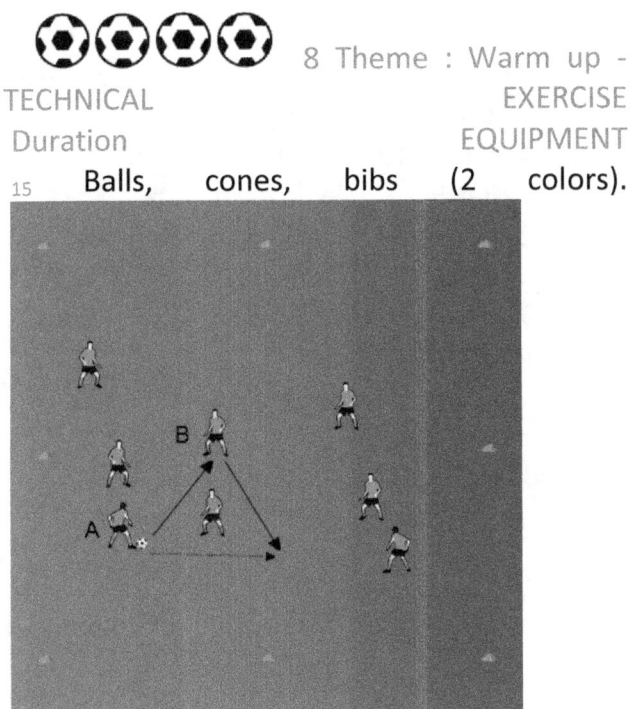

8 Theme : Warm up - EXERCISE

TECHNICAL

Duration EQUIPMENT

15 Balls, cones, bibs (2 colors).

Explanations

4 vs 4: two teams of 4 players play against each other on a 20x20 square meter field. Keeping possession of the ball. Trying to play 1-2 with their teammates. One point scored per 1-2 correctly made.

Example : A passes to B who passes back
to him (1-2). A gets the ball back after going
around an opponent.

Objectives

- One-two
- Pass and move
- Asking for the ball
- Ask for a lead pass

INSTRUCTIONS

- Pass and ask for the ball
- Pass and accelerate
- Focus when passing

VARIATIONS

- Add a joker who plays with the team in possession
- Add a second ball

Dribbling game

60 **U6-U11**

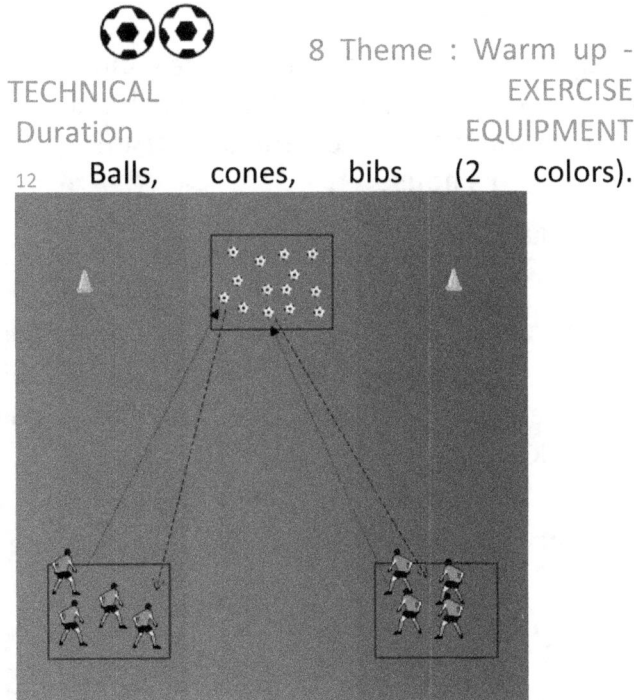

8 Theme : Warm up -

TECHNICAL   EXERCISE

Duration   EQUIPMENT

12   **Balls,   cones,   bibs   (2   colors).**

Explanations

Two teams of four (or more) players. Each team has a house (5x5 sq. m.). 15 m. away from the two houses is an aera containing all the balls.

The players wait in their house until the signal to start is given. Then the players run to get the balls and dribble them back to their house. When there are no more balls left, the team with the most balls in its house is the winner. Do several rounds.

VARIATIONS

• Players must first go around the cone
• Select one or more thieves for each team who are allowed to steal the balls from the other team's house

Objectives

•   Dribbling
•   Stopping   the   ball
•   Keeping   control   of   the   ball
INSTRUCTIONS
•   A   ball   at   a   time   per   player
• Passes are prohibited

First touch + Pass

61 **U9-U15**

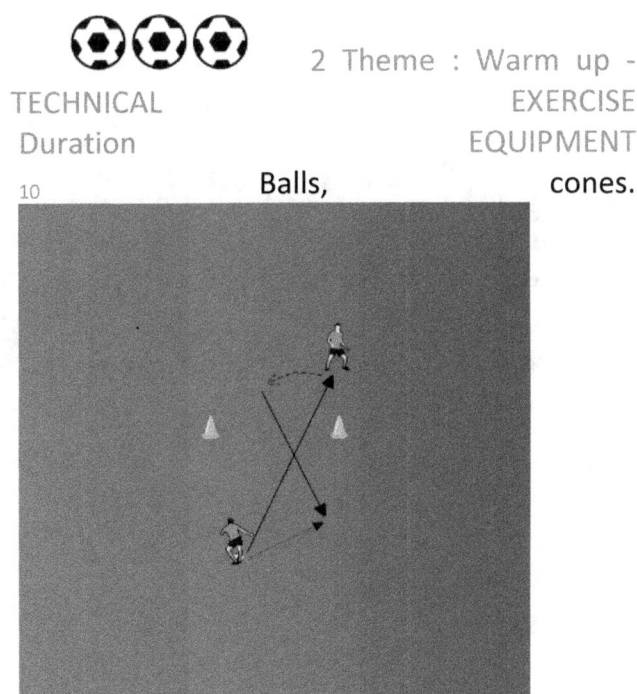

2 Theme : Warm up -
TECHNICAL   EXERCISE
Duration   EQUIPMENT
10   **Balls,**   **cones.**

Explanations

One ball/two players. Place the cones 1 1/2 meters apart to form a meter goal.
 One on one game. The players stand at an equal distance on either side of this meter

143

goal and make passes to each other with the ball always going between the cones.
A player passing the ball to hard loses one point.

Objectives

- First   touch
- Pass
- Accuracy

INSTRUCTIONS

- All passes have to stay on the ground and go between   the   cones
- Players have to use two touches (first touch and   pass)
- Each mistake gives the opponent one point

VARIATIONS

- Use the weak foot
- Reduce the distance between the cones
- Work with another partner

Give and go+ running techniques

62 U9+

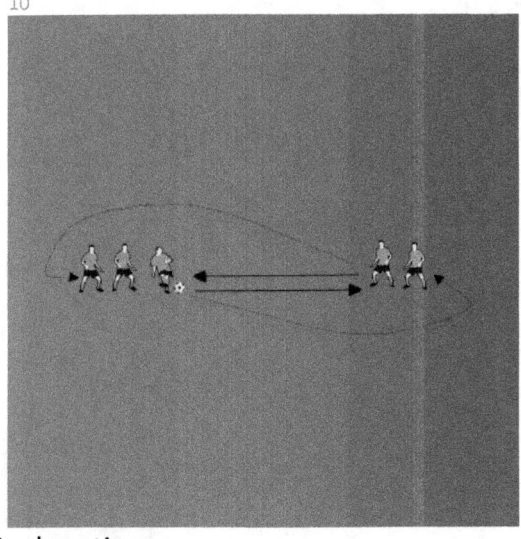

5 Theme : Warm up - EXERCISE

TECHNICAL

Duration   EQUIPMENT

10   Balls.

Explanations

Groups of 5 players with one ball per group. Give and go. The trainer announces running techniques after passes.

INSTRUCTIONS

Running   techniques   :

- high   knees
- heel-butt   touches
-   shuffle
-   etc.

VARIATIONS
- First   touch   +   Pass
- One-touch   pass

Objectives
-   Pass
- First   touch
- One-touch   play
- Running techniques

One-touch pass

63U9+

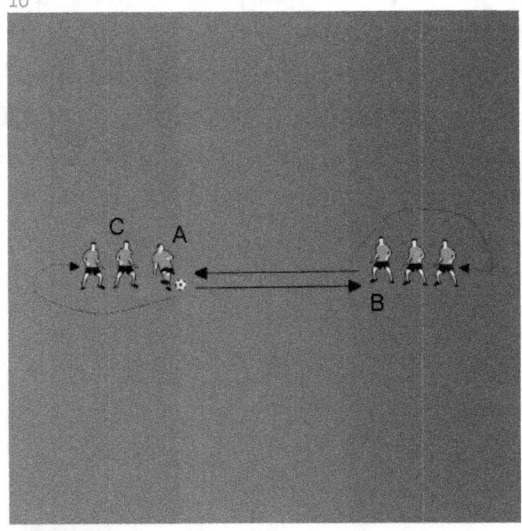

6 Theme : Warm up - EXERCISE

TECHNICAL

Duration   EQUIPMENT

10   **Balls.**

Explanations

Groups of 6 players (see diagram).
A passes the ball to B and runs back to their line.
B passes to C with one touch and runs back to their line; etc.

147

Passes must be precise and measured out to give rhythm to the game.

INSTRUCTIONS

- One-touch
- Be on your toes
- Attack the ball

VARIATIONS

Objectives

- Pass
- One-touch play
- Finesse ball touch
- Vary running techniques when running : backward, forward, shuffle, etc.
- Go around opposite group of players before running back to position

One-touch pass

64U9+

6 Theme : Warm up - EXERCISE

TECHNICAL

Duration

EQUIPMENT

10

Balls, discs.

Explanations

Players evolve in a 20x20 square meter field. Half of the players have a ball.
Players with a ball dribble and pass to players without a ball who pass back to them

149

with one touch to their feet.
Changing roles regularly.

VARIATIONS

• Passes and return passes played with weaker foot
• Double return pass : A dribbles then passes to a player B (without ball) ; B passes back to A who re- turns it to B ; B dribbles and tries to find a player without ball

Objectives

• Dribbling
• Pass
• One-touch return pass

INSTRUCTIONS

• Accurate and soft touch passes
• Players without ball jog
• Focus on the quality of the one-touch passes

1-2 (3)

EXERCISE Age difficultY Players

6 Theme : Warm up -

TECHNICAL   EXERCISE

Duration   EQUIPMENT

10   **Balls,**   **discs.**

Explanations

Players evolve in a 30x20 meter field. Half of the players have a ball.

Ball carriers play 1-2 with players without a ball.

A passes to B and asks for the ball, sprinting; B makes a lead pass with one touch.

If, after his pass, A doesn't ask for the ball, B controls it and becomes a ball carrier.

Objectives

- One-two
- Asking for the ball
- One-touch return pass

INSTRUCTIONS

- Accurate and soft touch passes
- Players without ball jog and ask for the ball
- Focus on the quality of the one-touch passes

VARIATIONS

- Both players score 1 point if the 1-2 is played around a third player

Big warm up game

66U11+

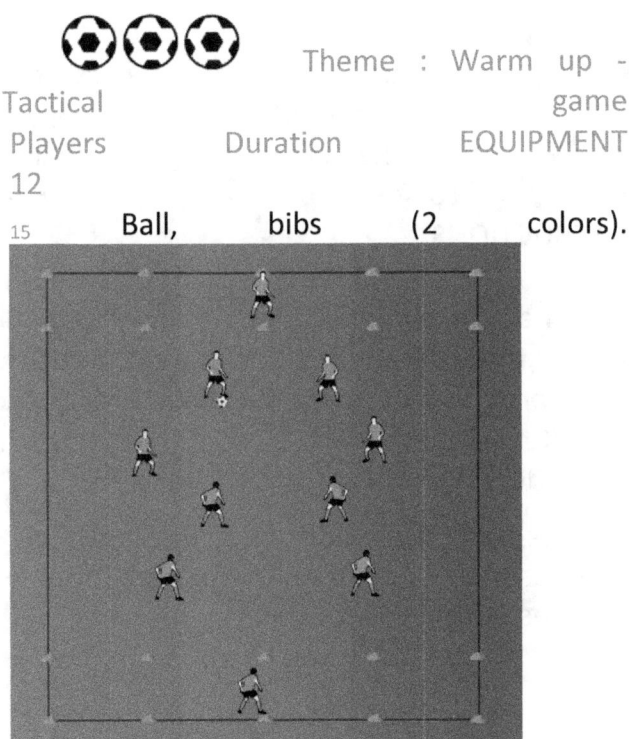

Theme : Warm up - Tactical game

Players   Duration   EQUIPMENT

12

15   Ball,   bibs   (2   colors).

Explanations

60x40 meter field with areas at the extremities. Two teams play against each other (6v6 or more) depending on the number of players. Keepers are in the zone opposed to their camp.

To score, the keeper has to catch an air pass without releasing it.

Objectives

- Ball   possession
- Forward   play
- Keeper   throw
- Long   air   pass

INSTRUCTIONS

- Free   play
- After a goal and when there is a goal kick, the keeper throws the ball for the other team
- No corner kick (throw from the keeper to the opposite   team)

VARIATIONS

- Passes from one's side are prohibited
- Passes from opposite's side are prohibited
- Passes with weak foot only

Big warm up game (2)

EXERCISE Age difficultY Players

67 U13+

⚽⚽⚽⚽ 12 Theme : Warm up -

Tactical   game

Duration   EQUIPMENT

15   **Balls,**   discs.

Explanations

50x30 meter field with areas at the extremities.

6 vs 6 stop-ball (or more depending on the number of players). To score, stop the ball in the zone opposed to one's camp.

155

Players don't wear pinnies. Well determining teams before the start of the game.

INSTRUCTIONS

- Free play
- Information gathering

VARIATIONS

Objectives

- Losing one's marker
- Forward play
- Receive a passe from a teammate in the in-goal to score

4 versus 2 keep-away

EXERCISE Age difficultY Players

68 U11+

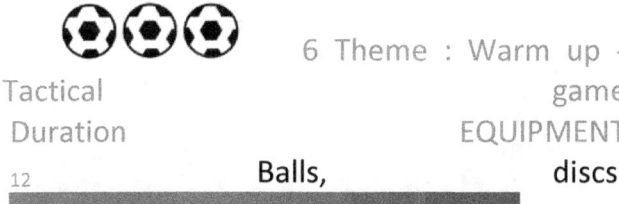

6 Theme : Warm up - game

Tactical

Duration EQUIPMENT

12 **Balls,** discs.

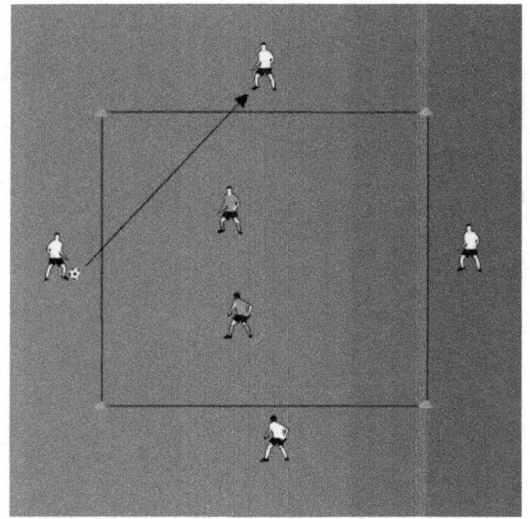

Explanations

12x12 meter field. Four players are outside of the field and try to keep possession of the ball. Two defenders are inside the field and try to intercept the ball.

157

The player who loses the ball becomes defend- er.

Objectives

- Passing
- Losing one's marker

INSTRUCTIONS

- Finding good pass angles
- 1 point scored by pass in the interval be- tween the 2 defenders

VARIATIONS

- Free play
- 2 touches maximum

8 versus 4 game

69U11+

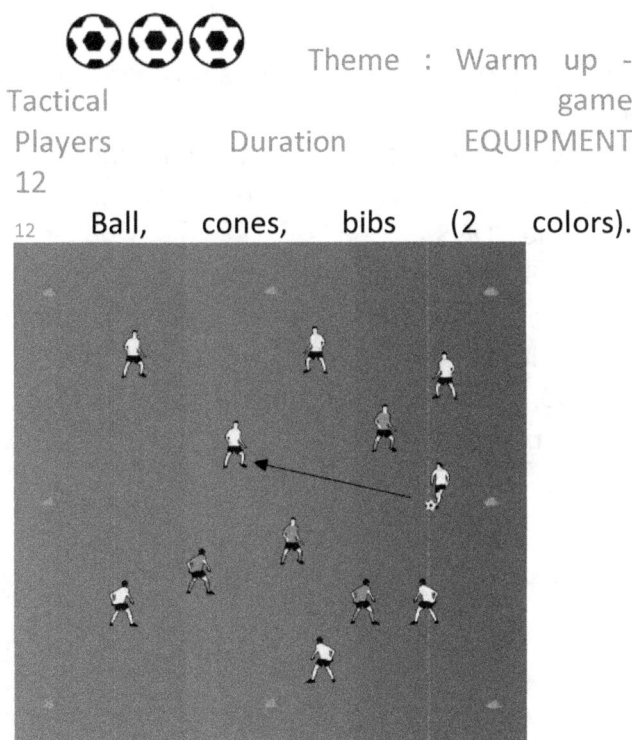

Theme : Warm up - Tactical   game

Players   Duration   EQUIPMENT
12

12   Ball,   cones,   bibs   (2   colors).

Explanations

25x25 meter game. All the players are inside the field.
8 players try to keep possession of the ball against 4 players who try to get the ball back

and try to keep it.

Form 3 teams of 4 players. 2 teams play together against a third one for 4 minutes then change role.

Objectives

- Keeping possession of the ball when outnumbered
- Keeping possession of the ball under the pressure of the opponent

INSTRUCTIONS

- The 8 player team is limited to 2 touches
- Free play for the 4 players team

VARIATIONS

- 1 point scored everytime a team makes 6 passes in a row

Door game

70 **U9+**

difficultY	Players	Duration	EQUIPMENT

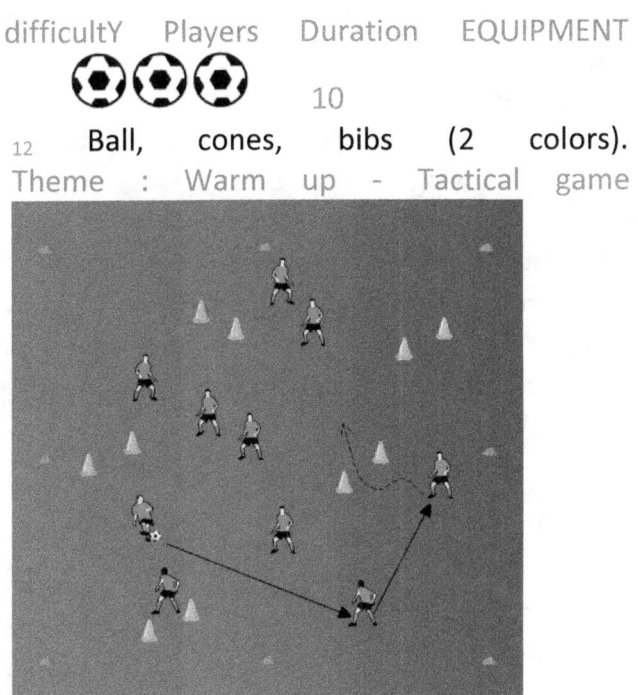

10

12 **Ball, cones, bibs (2 colors).**
Theme : Warm up - Tactical game

Explanations

40x30 meter field with small doors (2 meters).
5 vs 5 game (or more depending on the number of players). To score, dribble the ball through one of the doors.

After a goal, the play is still on but it is forbid- den to score twice in a row on the same door.

INSTRUCTIONS
- Head's up
- Help the ball carrier

VARIATIONS

Objectives
- Information gathering
- Losing one's marker
- Dribbling
- Set up doors of different colors (2 points if you score on a blue door; 3 points on a yellow door; etc.)
- 1 bonus point if a team scores 4 times in a row

Ball possession

71 U11+

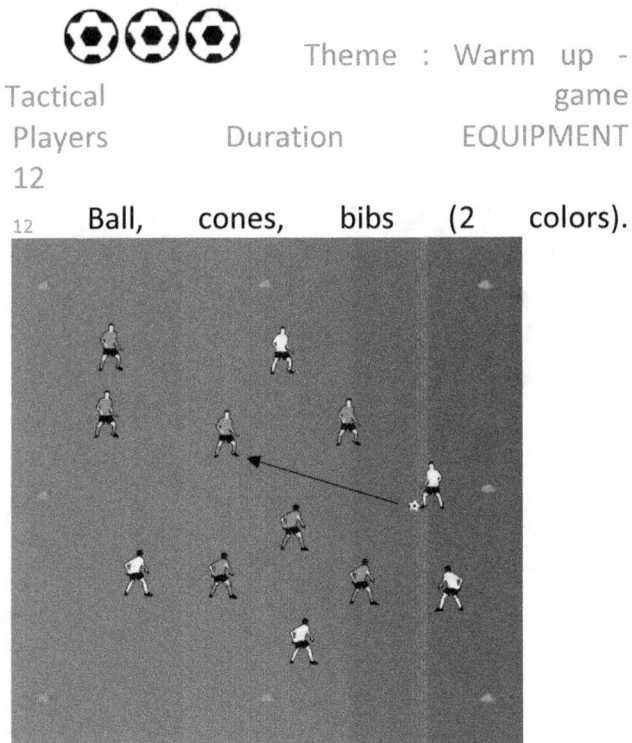

Theme : Warm up - Tactical game

Players Duration EQUIPMENT
12

12 Ball, cones, bibs (2 colors).

Explanations

Two teams of 6 players play against each other on a 40x35 meter field.
 Two neutral players always play with the team that has the ball.

163

1 point scored after 7 consecutive passes with- out losing possession of the ball. Changing neutral players regularly.

INSTRUCTIONS

- Head's up
- Help the ball carrier

VARIATIONS

Objectives

- Losing one's marker
- Pass
- First touch
- After 7 consecutive passes, each extra pass gives one point

Big warm up game (3)

EXERCISE Age difficultY Players

72 U13+

11 Theme : Warm up -
Tactical   game
Duration   EQUIPMENT
15   Ball,   cones,   bibs   (2   colors).

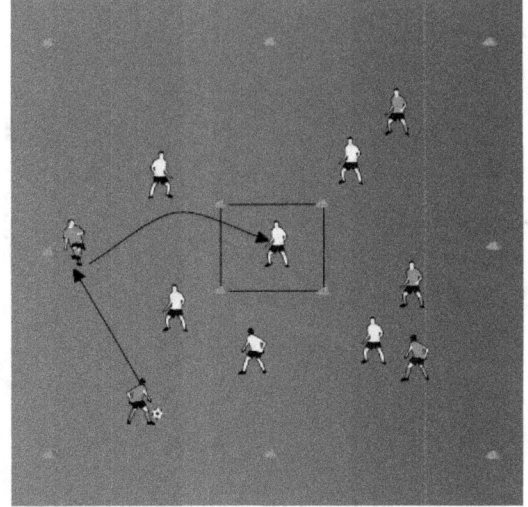

Explanations

An 8x8 meter area is in the middle of a 25x25 square meter field.

5 vs 5 game (or more depending on the number of players). The keeper is in the middle area. No other player is allowed to step in the

middle area.

To score, one has to pass the ball in the air to the keeper who has to catch the ball without releasing it. The keeper always plays with the team that has the ball.

VARIATIONS

• Free play
• Limiting the number of touches
• Pass to the goalkeeper on the ground are allowed

Objectives

•   Long   air   pass
•   Game   for   goalkeepers
INSTRUCTIONS
• The player who scores a goal becomes goalie
• Scoring with weak foot gives 2 points

One-touch return pass and trappings

EXERCISE Age difficultY Players

73U9+

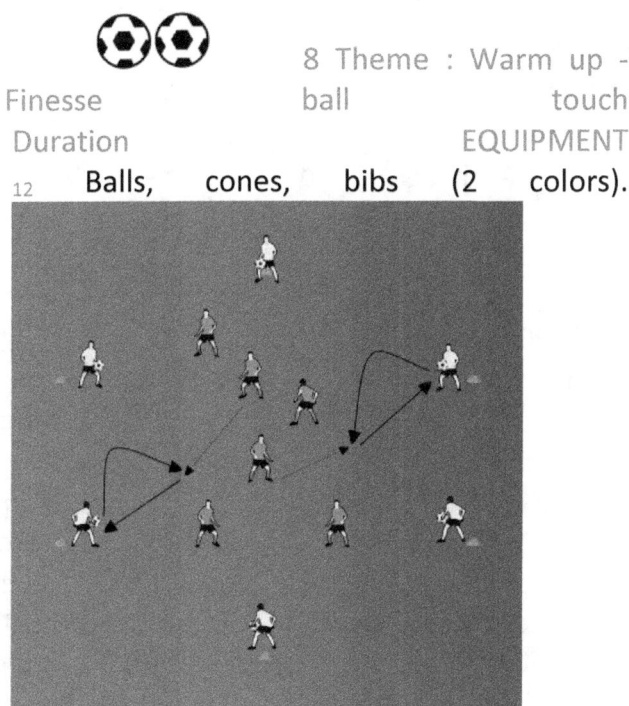

8 Theme : Warm up -
Finesse   ball   touch
Duration   EQUIPMENT
12 Balls,   cones,   bibs   (2   colors).

Explanations

Form two groups of players, the yellows and
the reds. Each member of the yellows has
a ball and they form a circle (about 15 m. in
diameter). The reds are inside the circle and
do not have a ball.

The reds jog around and ask for balls from the yellows. They use whatever technical sequence the trainer has asked for.

Use both feet. For air balls, the yellows throw the ball with their hands.

The reds and the yellows change roles every 2 minutes.

VARIATIONS

Objectives

- Asking for the ball
- One-touch return pass
- Trapping
- Pass

INSTRUCTIONS

• One-touch return pass (ball on the ground)
• One-touch return pass on air ball (volleying, heading)
• Chest trap and pass with the foot
• Etc.
• The players change roles after each sequence: Yellow passes to Red who returns it; then Yellow pass- es it back to Red with a single touch of the ball; then Red takes the place of Yellow

Juggling relay

74 U13+

3 Theme : Warm up - touch

Finesse   ball

Duration   EQUIPMENT

10   Balls,   cones.

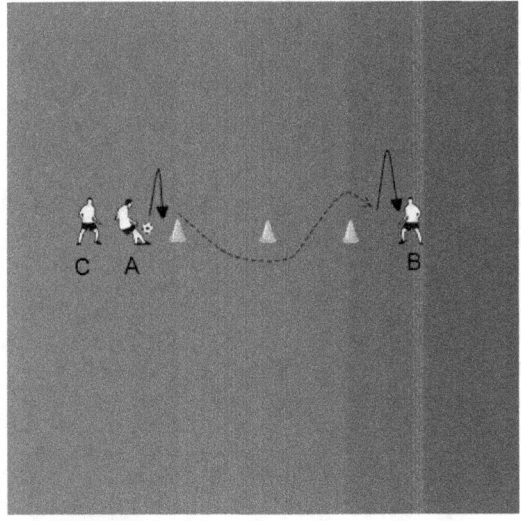

Explanations

Groups of 3 players with one ball per group. Team race relay.
 A juggles through the slalom and passes to B; B juggles through the slalom in the other way and passes to C; etc.

169

If the ball falls, the player restarts at the spot where the ball has fallen.

Objectives

- Controlling an air ball
- Improving the finesse ball touch
- Equilibre
- Coordination

INSTRUCTIONS
- FOcus on each touch of the ball
- Focus on the pass during the relay
- The fastest team wins: 3 passes per player. Do several rounds

VARIATIONS
- Restarting from the beginning if the ball falls
- Going around each cone

COORDINATION AND SUPPORT - RETURN PASS

EXERCIsE Age Difficulty

75 U9+

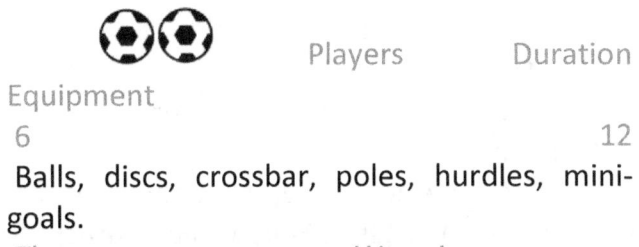

Players   Duration

Equipment

6   12

Balls, discs, crossbar, poles, hurdles, mini-goals.

Theme   :   Warming   up

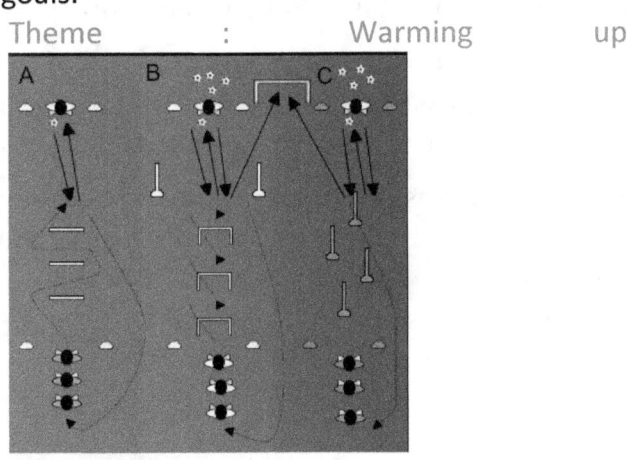

Explanations

Divide the players into 4 groups.
3 coordination stations followed by technical training and support-return pass.
The yellow players have the ball.
The yellows start as support passers.
Blue, white and red return to their respective

171

lines after each round.
Switch roles every 2 minutes.

Objectives

- Coordination
- Support work
- One touch ball passing
- Support and return pass

instructions

- A : Blue side steps between the slats and then returns the pass to Yellow in one touch

- B : White jumps over the hurdles with his feet joined, passes to Yellow in one touch and then scores in the mini-goal in one touch

- C : Red crosses the forest, passes to Yellow in one touch and then scores in one touch

variations

- Switch stations

TIC-TAC-TOE

Exercise Age Difficulty

76 U9+

Theme : Warming up

Players   Duration   Equipment
6   15

Balls, discs, hoops, crossbars, cones, bibs (2 colors).

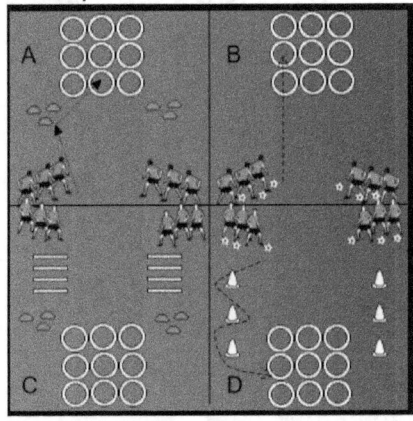

Explanations

Here are several variations of the football ver - sion of the tic-tac-toe game. Make teams of 3 or 4 players.

One after the other, the players of each team will place a pinny in a hoop.

The first team to line up 3 bibs wins.

When all the players have passed and no one has won, you can move one pinny at a time.

Objectives

- Speed
- Coordination
- Dribbling
- Thought process
- Competition

instructions

- Many possible variants
- Vary the coordination stations
- Add challenges to the ball control: only use weak foot, add obstacles, etc.

variations

- A: Place 3 bibs for each team next to the grid. Run to place a bib
- B: one ball per player. Dibble the ball to place it in one of the hoops
- C: same as A but do a little coordination work before placing a bib
- D: same as B but do a small slalom before placing the ball

DRIBBLING, PASSING and return pass

77 U11+

Players   Duration

Equipment

10

12   **Balls,   discs,   bibs.**

Theme   :   FUNDAMENTAL   SKILLS

Explanations

Surface area of 20x20m. 4 blues without balls in the middle of each side.
 6 reds each have a ball and dribble it into the field.
 The drill evolves according to the instructions given by the coach.
 Change roles.

Objectives

-                                 Dribbling
-                                      Pass
-      Support   and   return   pass
-           First   touch

instructions

- Dribble the ball forward, leave it to a blue and take his place
- Dribble the ball forward, pass it to a blue and take his place
- Play as support passer with a blue and continue dribbling the ball forward
- Play a screen with a blue coming to meet him, leave him the ball and take his place

variations

- Other instructions
- Perform an action at the coach's whistle
- Other: red makes his move when a blue player is available

4 VERSUS 4 CONES GAME

Exercise Age Difficulty

78 **U7-U15**

Players   Duration

Equipment

8

20 **Balls, discs, cones, bibs (2 colors).**
Theme   :   SMALL   SIDED   GAMES

Explanations

Surface area of 25x25m. Place 10 cones in 2 opposite corners.
4 on 4 game.
When a player tips over a cone from the opposing team, he picks it up and puts it in his corner. He adds it to the cones that are

already there.
At the end of the game, the team with the most cones in its corner wins.

Objectives

- Small sided teams
- Reduced surface area
- Shooting at a target

instructions

- Players can knock down several cones at the same time
- Forbidden to knock down cones with their feet
- A player bringing back a cone to his corner is not part of the game

variations

- Cones of different colors: a yellow cone is worth 3 points; a green cone 5 points
- Let the knocked down cones on the ground: the team that knocks down all the opposing cones wins

FINISHING SKILLS

79 **U13+**

Theme : SCORING GOALS

Players   Duration   Equipment

16

20 **Balls, discs, bibs (4 colors), 2 goals..**

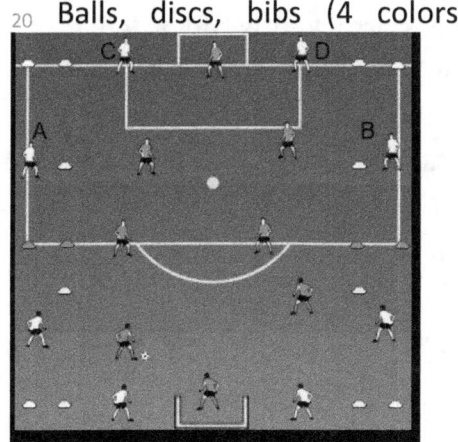

Explanations

Size of the field is 2 penalty areas.
Form 4 teams of 4 players.
Two teams play against each other. The players of the 2 teams who do not play are lateral or offensive supports.

Objectives

-            Score   goals
- Use   lateral   and   offensive   supports
- Take advantage of the numerical superiority to   score
- Risk   taking   when   facing   the   goal instructions

- When the reds attack, the 2 whites (A and B) and 2 yellows (C and D) of the offensive zone serve as support.

- When the blues attack, it is the other 2 white and yellow players who become the offensive support

- Supports cannot score or play together variations

- Support players are limited to 2 ball touches
- Support players is limited to 1 ball touch
- Support players can play together but not score
- The last defender plays goalkeeper